moments of glory

MOSES

...feet of clay

GENE A. GETZ

A Division of G/L Publications
Glendale, California, U.S.A.

Other good Regal reading by Gene A. Getz:
The Measure of a Church
The Measure of a Man
The Measure of a Woman
The Measure of a Family
Abraham: Trials and Triumphs
David: God's Man in Faith and Failure
Joshua: Defeat to Victory

The foreign language publishing of all Regal books is under the direction of GLINT. GLINT provides financial and technical help for the adaptation, translation and publishing of books in more than 85 languages for millions of people worldwide.

For more information write: GLINT, 110 W. Broadway, Glendale, CA 91204.

The Scripture quotations in this publication are from the *New American Standard Bible*. © The Lockman Foundation 1960, 1962, 1963, 1968, 1971. Used by permission.

Fourth Printing, 1980

Published by
Regal Books Division, G/L Publications
Glendale, California 91209
Printed in U.S.A.

Library of Congress Catalog Card No. 75-23519

ISBN 0-8307-0400-0

CONTENTS

ACKNOWLEDGMENTS

I would like to express my gratitude to Dr. Kenneth Barker, Professor of Semitic Languages and Old Testament Exegesis at Dallas Theological Seminary. Dr. Barker first read and evaluated my original manuscript and offered several very helpful suggestions. His comment after reading the material served as a real source of encouragement to me personally—especially since I respect very highly his depth of scholarship and the quality of his Christian life-style. Said he: "I never really appreciated Moses until reading this manuscript. He faced almost *everything*, didn't he?"

Thanks, Ken!

GARY GONZALES

study for several reasons:

First, as we've already seen, he was one of God's *greatest* servants.

Second, we know a lot about Moses primarily because God chose to record an abundance of information about his total life.

And third, Moses was a human being like you and me.

Along with Moses' strengths are recorded his *weaknesses*. From Scripture we can discover his *achievements* as well as his *failures*. There is *no* Christian living today who cannot identify with Moses and learn how to be an individual whom God can use.

MOSES' PARENTS
an example to follow

As a parent, have you ever faced a serious crisis with your children—one so great you didn't know where to turn or what to do? Amram and Jochebed, Moses' parents, faced such a crisis! But they knew where to turn and what to do! And their actions teach all of us a tremendous lesson—whether we are parents or not.

Moses was conceived during a time of great stress for Israel. The prospect of his birth placed his parents in an extremely difficult position. The problem they faced was gigantic and awesome.

THE BACKGROUND OF THE PROBLEM

The story of Moses is a continuation, a sequel to that of Joseph. Joseph was one of the 12 sons of Jacob. Because he was a favorite son of Jacob and severely hated by his brothers, he was sold as a slave and transported to Egypt. Eventually, through a series of God-led events, he rose from slavery to the position of prime minister. In this significant position he prepared the people of Egypt for a great famine, so widespread that it also affected his family back in

Canaan. Because Joseph was respected by Pharaoh, his whole family, consisting of 70 people, was brought to Egypt. Here they settled on a beautiful and fertile section of land where they could live in peace and plenty (see Gen. 45:16-20).

But life was not always to be one of tranquility and rest for the children of Israel. Time has a way of blurring memories, changing circumstances and the hearts of men. And the children of Israel were not exempt from this process.

Multiplication of Israel

For nearly 400 years "the sons of Israel were fruitful and increased greatly, and multiplied, and became exceedingly mighty, so that the land was filled with them" (Exod. 1:7). From the small beginning of 70 souls, they became a great nation—probably numbering in excess of two million. But, as is so often true in life, what sometimes begins as a great blessing can also become a great problem—even a curse.

And 400 years is a long time! Joseph's exploits were forgotten, "lost" in the continuing events of history. And so was Pharaoh's promise to Israel. In fact, "a new king arose over Egypt, who did not know Joseph" (1:8).

No doubt the phrase, "a new king," meant a leader who differed substantially in his approach to ruling the people. He seemingly departed from his predecessors' policies and principles. In fact, the text implies he was not interested in the "way" the previous kings ruled Egypt. Thus, when the Scriptures read that this king "did not know Joseph," it is clearly implied that he could "care less" about the man

11

whose name had been a household word in the archives of Egypt. This "new king" was interested in building a reputation for *himself*, not in perpetuating the exploits of his predecessor—especially those of a Jew named Joseph.

The new king's attitude towards Israel's growth rate gives us insight into his personality. He was a threatened man! And, in true "threatened style," he exaggerated and projected his fears for all to see: "Behold," he exclaimed, "the people of the sons of Israel are more and mightier than we" (1:9).

Pharaoh's concern was really twofold. First, if there was a war, Israel might join the enemies of Egypt. And second, if this should happen, Israel might eventually leave Egypt (1:10). Interestingly, Pharaoh wasn't comfortable living *with the Israelites* nor was he comfortable living *without them*.

But, his bizarre behavior—directed primarily by emotion rather than clear thinking—was yet to reach its zenith as he developed what he felt was a necessary counterattack.

Mobilization Against Israel

Pharaoh's attack came in three stages; not in logical thought-through phases but, rather, in emotional bombardments. In the first stage he tried to demoralize the Israelites and make them so weary that they would become nonproductive. Pharaoh "appointed taskmasters over them to afflict them with hard labor" (Exod. 1:11).

Theoretically, hard work was supposed to cut down the birthrate. But not so for the Israelites. The harder they worked, the more children they produced. So we read: "The more they afflicted them, the more they multiplied and the more they spread out" (1:12).

And, as the threat level rose, so did the king's hostility. Pressure, already abnormal, took on almost unbearable proportions. The Egyptian taskmasters "made their lives bitter with hard labor in mortar and bricks and at all kinds of labor in the field" (1:14).

But all of this was to no avail. Israel continued to grow and expand. Consequently, Pharaoh initiated the second stage. It was a wicked and terrible plan, one that could only be derived in the heart of a ruthless, egotistical man who was terribly weak on the inside and all facade on the outside. He came up with a plan to kill all the newborn sons of Israel.

Somewhat hidden in this scheme was a very subtle strategy. Obviously one way to limit the birthrate was to decrease the number of males—kill off the aggressors. However, we might also conclude that stage two was an extension of the demoralization approach. If hard work wouldn't stop procreation, perhaps the ruthless destruction of the male offspring would. Who would feel free to bring a child in the world under a 50/50 probability of losing him?

But again the plot failed! The midwives who were ordered by the king to kill all the male children at birth were more loyal to God than to the king of Egypt (1:15-17). Though they told only a half-truth when confronted by the king, God still honored the deeper motives of their hearts. They took a chance, risking their own lives, and tried to be true to the light they had. Consequently, God honored and blessed them (1:18-21).

Pharaoh's most ignominious and irrational act was yet to come. In a final frenzied third stage he ordered every newborn male to be "cast into the Nile" (1:22). Imagine the weeping and wailing among the families of Israel as newborn infants were snatched from their mothers' breasts and thrown into the murky waters of the Nile.

It was in the midst of this severe crisis in Egypt that a little boy, later called Moses, was born. And it was in the midst of this crisis that we see a family face a terrifying situation head on—with *faith*, *courage* and a unique *strategy* that by contrast made Pharaoh's behavior stand out for what it was: emotional, ego-centric, fearful and irrational.

HOW MOSES' PARENTS FACED THE PROBLEM

The record of Moses' birth and preservation in Exodus 2:1-10 presents almost exclusively the human factors involved in this event. But there is a divine dimension interwoven into the account that is really only visible through the lens of the New Testament. While the focus of the Old Testament account zeros in on Moses' parents, the writer of the book of Hebrews shows us a divine perspective that guarded the hearts and minds of Moses' parents even after the people of God had lived for 400 years in a pagan and polytheistic environment.

They Had Faith

"*By faith* Moses, when he was born, was hidden for three months by his parents" (Heb. 11:23, italics added).

Very little space is given in Scripture to describe Moses' parents. But what is recorded, though succinctly and simply stated, reveals, through content and implication, the depth of their relationship with the God of Israel.

Moses' father's name was Amram, and his mother's name was Jochebed (Exod. 6:20). Both were of the tribe of Levi and both were reared in an environment that was virtually opposed to *all* that God had ever revealed to their forefathers.

Evidently, the whole nation of Israel, after 400 years of direct exposure to the heathen deities and practices of Egypt, were steeped in the same attitudes and behavior. This is why Joshua, many years later, charged a succeeding generation to "fear the Lord" and to "put way the gods" which their fathers worshiped and served in Egypt (Josh. 24:14). How firmly entrenched these religious practices of Egypt must have been in the hearts and minds of Israel to reappear in their children many years later—even after God had manifested Himself and revealed His law at Mount Sinai.

Through all of this Moses' parents had somehow remained true to the God of Israel. So when Moses was born in the midst of a great crisis, his parents believed that God would preserve his life.

They Had Courage

Closely aligned with faith is *courage*. And, according to the New Testament record, Moses' parents had both: "They were not afraid of the king's edict" (Heb. 11:23).

Obviously they had a lot to be afraid of. At any

moment the child could have been snatched away from Jochebed and cast into the Nile.

Imagine those first three months! For nearly 100 days they hid their beautiful child and guarded his crib. They nursed him regularly to avoid the hunger pangs that would cause him to cry out and reveal his hiding place, bringing sudden death. What faith and courage!

They Had a Strategy

But the time came when they could no longer hide Moses. The quiet, peaceful little baby began to take on the characteristics of a normal, active and growing child. The danger of discovery became too great. It was time to take action.

Between the lines of Scripture there appears to be a strategy so unique that it could be conceived only by people whose minds were guided by God Himself and whose hearts were free from anxiety and emotional reaction. Ordinarily those about to be trapped would panic. But not Moses' parents.

Notice their tactic! Carefully and cautiously Jochebed tarred a small basket so that it was waterproof. She placed the baby in the basket and took him directly to the very means of death itself—the Nile (Exod. 2:3). That which was the place of death became the hope for life. Soldiers would never look for babies in the river—especially the Nile.

Perhaps Jochebed chose the Nile because she knew that Pharaoh's daughter came there regularly to bathe. Why not put the child where he would be found by the only one who could save him—the daughter of the king who issued the death edict?

16

Perhaps the princess would be attracted to little Moses and his beauty just as his true parents had been (2:2).

Sure enough! If this *was* the plan, it worked. And right on schedule. When Pharaoh's daughter saw the child, after he had been taken from the river, she recognized him immediately as one of the Hebrew children, knew why he was there and "had pity on him" (2:6).

At this point, the second step was taken in the parents' strategy. As Pharaoh's daughter looked down at the hungry, crying little babe and wondered what to do next, Miriam—Moses' sister—suddenly appeared and offered a solution. "Shall I go and call a nurse for you from the Hebrew women?" she asked (2:7).

Coincidence? I don't think so. Human reactions are often easy to predict. If this was a strategy—carefully and cautiously contrived for three months —it was working beautifully.

The result, of course, is ironic, almost humorous. Miriam brought Jochebed, Moses' mother, who took back her little boy to nurse and rear for several years. And she did it all with the protection of the daughter of the king of Egypt, the same king who had ordered Moses' death! Even more ironic, Jochebed was paid to mother her own child! (see 2:9).

THE TWENTIETH-CENTURY HOME

What can a story like this, so far removed from our culture and experience, teach us *today*?

First of all, the early years of Moses' life had a great influence on his thinking and attitudes. Even though

17

he grew up in a pagan environment, those first four or five years in his parents' home, before he went to live in the king's palace, left an imprint on him for life. He never was able to forget God and his own people.

The application is obvious. As parents, or future parents, do you realize how important your influence is in the early years of your child's life? It's not so much what you *teach* him, but rather what you *are*— your actions, your attitudes, even your tone of voice! A child who observes parents who love God, who love each other and who love their neighbors as themselves can never get away from that influence!

Second, a pagan culture, no matter how degenerate, need not destroy our children. But to combat these negative influences we need the same factors in our lives as Moses' parents had:

We must have *faith* in God—faith that He will help us and help our children become followers of Jesus Christ.

We must have *courage*—boldness to stand against the waves of materialism, secularism and sensualism that are bombarding our children every day.

We must have a *strategy*. Faith and courage are but the foundations upon which we must build. We'll never rescue our children from Satan's plot to destroy them by merely trusting God. We must *act* on our faith!

How do you measure up to these biblical criteria? Have you combined faith, courage and a strategy to bring up your children "in the discipline and instruction of the Lord" (Eph. 6:4)? This can be accomplished only in the home. The church and Christian schools can only assist. They can only build upon a parental foundation.

Remember! It is never too late to begin; though it is more difficult when the children are older.

LIFE RESPONSE

What can you do to take the first step—right now —in better preparing your children to follow Jesus Christ?

Parents: As a husband and wife, compare notes with each other. What steps can you take together to develop a strategy that will achieve the goal of effective family nurture?

Children: Cooperate with your parents, no matter what your age, as they attempt to follow through on this project. Remember the words of Paul: "Children, obey your parents in the Lord, for this is right. Honor your father and mother (which is the first commandment with a promise), that it may be well with you, and that you may live long on the earth" (Eph. 6:1-3).

MOSES'
significant choice

Have you ever had to make a decision that would affect the direction of your life? Moses had to make a decision like that! And even though it was a painful decision, it was the right decision. Had he not made it, he would have walked directly out of the will of God!

Moses was born during a time of great stress for Israel. But, in spite of the fact that his little life could have been snuffed out at any moment, what appeared to be an almost inevitable crisis turned into unusual advantages for Moses. Both his heredity and environment blended in a unique way to set Moses apart, first among the Egyptians and then among his own people, the children of Israel.

But with advantage comes tremendous responsibility. From those to whom God gives much, He expects much (see Luke 12:48). And, as we'll see in this chapter, Moses' insight and awareness of this truth led him to face some very difficult decisions in his later life.

20

MOSES' HERITAGE AND ACHIEVEMENTS IN HIS EARLY LIFE

For the most part, Moses had very little to do with his heritage and the opportunities for achievement which surrounded him during his life. All he had to do was to take advantage of these opportunities and turn them into outstanding achievements.

His early life was characterized by three significant dimensions that put him, both literally and figuratively, "head and shoulders" above his peers. These were: 1) outstanding physical assets; 2) unusual intellectual accomplishments; and 3) exceptional leadership ability.

> "And it was at this time that Moses was born; and he was lovely in the sight of God; and he was nurtured three months in his father's home. And after he had been exposed, Pharaoh's daughter took him away, and nurtured him as her own son. And Moses was educated in all the learning of the Egyptians, and he was a man of power in words and deeds" (Acts 7:20-22).

His Physical Assets

At times, a child is born into this world that, from the moment of birth, is a striking specimen of humanity. Moses was such a child, and the writers of Scripture seem to emphasize this point. In the Old Testament account of his birth, we read that his mother recognized that "he was *beautiful*" (Exod. 2:2). In the New Testament, the writer of the book of Hebrews included both parents in his tribute. They both recognized that "he was a *beautiful* child" (Heb. 11:23).

Stephen, however, in the classic sermon that resulted in his martyrdom, added a divine dimension to this tribute: "And it was at this time [the time of great stress and persecution] that Moses was born; and he was *lovely* in the sight of God" (Acts 7:20).

We know, of course, that as a general rule "man looks at the outward appearance, but the Lord looks at the heart" (1 Sam. 16:7). And in Moses' case we see that he inherited unusual inner qualities which characterized his personality and made him "lovely in the sight of God." He also inherited outstanding external qualities that made him a physically attractive person in the sight of man as well. When you combine these two dimensions you have an outstanding candidate for winning both the "Mr. Egypt" and the "Mr. Israel" award, so to speak.

Josephus records in his reputable history of the Jews that Moses as a young man was so outstanding in his physical features that the Egyptians would often try to catch a glimpse of him—just to see what this man looked like. And some, who were privileged to "take a long look," would often stare at him, finding it hard to turn their eyes away from this unusual young man. Being the "son of Pharaoh's daughter" and the only apparent heir to the king's throne, of course, added to this intrigue.

His Intellectual Accomplishments

When Moses eventually left his Jewish home, probably at about age four or five, and went to live in the king's court, he began an educational career that was second to none in the pagan world. Stephen informs us that he "was educated in all the learning of the Egyptians" (Acts 7:22). This means he became a scholar.

No doubt Moses came close to being one of the most educated young men in all of Egypt. Who would have greater opportunity than the son of Pharaoh's daughter—this one who lived in the king's palace as part of the royal family and who had access to every educational opportunity and learning resource Egypt could offer? With free tuition, personalized instruction from the best scholars in the land, and an eager, inquiring young mind, Moses was destined to receive his "Ph.D." from the University of Egypt, graduating summa cum laude.

We can go even further in speculating and drawing conclusions about Moses' education. Egypt, at that time, represented one of the most productive and progressive countries in the world. The nation's social, economic and educational achievements were almost unprecedented. To this day, the pyramids stand as a tribute to the almost unbelievable achievements of the Egyptian architects and builders. These fascinating structures reflect mathematical insights, artistic skills and feats of engineering that are almost inconceivable for a culture that existed so many years ago. It is logical to conclude that Moses probably became one of the most educated young men in the world.

His Leadership Abilities

Moses was not just a theoretician, one who could fascinate other scholars by working out complicated mathematical formulas, or one who could use several foreign languages to spice up his lectures. Rather, his intellectual achievements were translated into life. As Stephen proclaimed, Moses was a man of both intellect and action: "He was a man of power in words and deeds" (Acts 7:22).

Obviously, Moses became an outstanding educator himself. What he knew, he could communicate to others. He had power with words. And this skill was manifest in his ability to command respect and to direct and lead people.

Josephus gives us reliable, though extra-biblical, information that illustrates Stephen's statement concerning Moses. He reports that when the Ethiopians attacked Egypt and were on the verge of defeating them, Moses was appointed general over the Egyptian army. Under his dynamic leadership, the Ethiopians were driven back and defeated. Moses was truly "a man of power in *words and deeds*."

MOSES' DELIBERATION AND DECISION IN LATER LIFE

Stephen, in Acts 7, clearly gave us some outstanding insights into Moses' early life. But somewhere along the way Moses began to understand that there was more to life than being the center of attention and rising to a place of prominence in Egypt. No doubt the early years of Moses' life in his parents' home, where he was exposed both to the hardships of slavery and bondage and to their faith in the God of Israel, never faded from his memory. For, as he traveled about the land, riding overland in a golden chariot or cruising up and down the Nile in the king's

24

private barge, the things he observed kept those memories alive.

In some respects what he saw was contradictory. He saw the same slavery and brutal treatment as before, but where now was the faith in the God of Abraham, Isaac and Jacob? All that was visible was a people who were worshiping the gods of Egypt. The God of Israel who had delivered Moses from a watery grave was no longer acknowledged by the majority of the people of Israel.

How and when these thoughts began to grip Moses, we do not know. Perhaps his inquiring mind and research findings led him to study his own heritage. Perhaps he quietly and secretly spent time talking with his true parents from whom he learned more about his people and their national and religious destiny. Or perhaps God spoke directly to Moses.

But whatever the method, Moses became aware of his Jewish heritage. And he learned that God had a special plan for his life and for Israel, a plan far different from the one that seemed to be unfolding in the mind of his foster mother.

Moses eventually came to the place where he had to make a decision—and a tough decision it was! He had to choose to identify with slaves and experience unusual suffering, or to maintain his identity with royalty and experience the pleasures of sin. The first choice would lead to an eternal reward; the other would result in an immediate reward and earthly benefits. Hebrews 11:24-26 makes it very clear which course Moses took:

"By faith Moses, when he had grown up,

refused to be called the son of Pharaoh's daughter; choosing rather to endure ill-treatment with the people of God, than to enjoy the passing pleasures of sin; considering the reproach of Christ greater riches than the treasures of Egypt; for he was looking to the reward."

Identity with Slavery Versus Identity with Royalty

No doubt Moses' decision was not made on the spur of the moment. He probably spent many agonizing days counting the cost. Being a sensitive man, his greatest concern would be his foster mother. Had she not saved his life? Had she not provided him with all of the advantages of an Egyptian education? Had she not given him the opportunity to become a great leader in Egypt? And had she not provided him with the chance that would possibly make him heir to the throne of Egypt?

Imagine the emotional agony he must have experienced when he announced to her one day that he no longer could be called "the son of Pharaoh's daughter." Imagine on the one hand her tears as she felt the stinging blow of rejection; and on the other hand her bitter words accusing Moses of being ungrateful and insensitive. It was a *hard* decision.

Humanly speaking, Moses' choice would result in great personal sacrifice: leaving a position of prominence to become a "nobody"; leaving a place of acceptance and honor for one of rejection and dishonor; leaving fame and fortune to become a servant without personal resources.

26

Yes, it was a hard decision, but Moses really had no choice. If he wanted to be in the will of God he *had* to identify with his own people. He *had* to reject his royal position. The very nature of the case made it an either/or decision.

The Pain of Suffering Versus the Pleasures of Sin

Emotional rejection is one thing; physical suffering is another. And Moses' decision meant both. He chose "to endure ill-treatment with the people of God" rather than "to enjoy the passing pleasures of sin" (Heb. 11:25).

The "pleasures of sin" refers to more than the personal enjoyment that comes from indulging the sensual appetites. Rather, the sin would be to deliberately choose to continue his identity with Egypt rather than Israel; to deliberately refuse to become the man God had chosen to help the Israelites out of their bondage; to deliberately walk away from the will of God and take the easy road rather than the difficult one. But Moses made the choice—a difficult choice. He had to obey God rather than man.

An Ultimate Spiritual Reward Versus an Immediate Earthly Reward

Why did Moses make this difficult decision? The writer of Hebrews makes it clear: He considered "the reproach of Christ greater riches than the treasures of Egypt; for he was looking to the reward" (Heb. 11:26).

Moses was already a rich man. From his childhood he had everything a person could ever want or dream

27

of. His royal garments were woven from exquisite fabrics. His food was the best Egypt could offer. His allowance was open-ended. Servants responded to his every demand. And, of course, if he remained in the royal court, he would eventually have an even greater inheritance—all the wealth of Egypt.

But Moses saw beyond the temporal and the material. He saw an eternal reward, a reward that would never fade away. And, even though his decision would mean rejection, poverty and suffering, he was willing to pay the price to inherit an eternal reward.

Moses, of course, knew little, if anything, about the future sufferings of Jesus Christ. But, by faith, Moses chose to endure what Christ Himself would endure when He also chose to leave His royal position in heaven to become a mere man and a servant, and to suffer death on the cross.

So the writer of Hebrews, with the perspective of history, identifies Moses' decision with the very decision Christ made when He chose to become like man in order to save man from his bondage to sin. Moses responded to the light he had. And, in so doing, he entered the Hebrew "hall of faith" along with other greats such as Abraham, Isaac, Jacob and Joseph.

MOSES' CHOICE AND
THE TWENTIETH-CENTURY CHRISTIAN

Humanly speaking, very few of us can truly identify with Moses in physical assets, intellectual accomplishments or leadership abilities. Nor can we identify with the situation which required him to make a decision of this kind. But though the literal

28

aspects of Moses' decision are unusual—giving up a royal position to become a slave, giving up the pleasures of Egypt to endure suffering with a tormented people, giving up a material inheritance to inherit an eternal reward—in essence, God asks every person who desires to live as a Christian to make the same basic decision.

There were people in Jesus' day who were not willing to make that decision. Position, pleasure and plenty stood in the way of becoming a follower of Jesus Christ. Consequently, Jesus made some startling statements that often jolted people!

For example, He said, "If anyone comes to Me, and does not hate his own father and mother and wife and children and brothers and sisters, yes, and even his own life, he cannot be My disciple" (Luke 14:26).

To read this statement superficially causes confusion. Jesus Christ is not justifying "hate," which He so specifically condemns in other passages. Rather, He is saying that no one can really follow Him, if others are *more important* than He is. Love for God must be first. Others must be second. And when we put God first, our relationships with family and friends and ourselves will come into proper focus. Our priority must always be God first and family second.

So in Moses' case, God had to come first; Pharaoh's daughter—his foster mother—had to be second. And, of course, in this instance he even had to refuse to be called her son, because to do so would be to identify with Egypt and its idolatry and sin against the God of Israel.

Another great stumbling block in Jesus' day was

wealth. A rich man came to Jesus one day and asked Him what he must do to inherit eternal life. Jesus said he should sell all that he had and give it to the poor. But, because he was a very wealthy man, he went away very grieved (see Matt. 19:16-22).

Again, some people have greatly misunderstood Jesus' statement. Obviously, no man can inherit eternal life by selling everything and giving it away. If he could, all of Scripture would be one great contradiction. For man can only be saved by grace through faith—not works.

This man of course missed the point. If he were truly interested in eternal life, if he were truly interested in putting God first in his life, he would have gladly pursued the conversation further. But Jesus knew what his problem was. Wealth was more important than God, and Jesus went right to the heart of the problem.

Again, Jesus was dealing with a priority. Jesus had said on another occasion: "But seek first His kingdom, and His righteousness; and all these things shall be added to you" (Matt. 6:33). So today, every man must face the same basic decision that Moses faced. Am I really willing to lose my life to find it again (Matt. 10:39)? Is there anything in my life that is more important than God?

LIFE RESPONSE

Following are examples of things that can be more important to us than God in the life of both a non-Christian as well as a Christian. If you are *not* a Christian these things may be keeping you from accepting Jesus Christ as your personal Saviour. If you *are* a Christian these things may be keeping you from enjoying God's fullest blessing in your life. Check the things that you feel are hindering your relationship with God, because you have put them before God in importance:

☐ Husband   ☐ Job
☐ Wife   ☐ Education
☐ Children   ☐ Hobbies
☐ Friends   ☐ Income
☐ Brothers/sisters   ☐ Savings
☐ Car   ☐ Sports
☐ Time   ☐ TV
☐ Life goals   ☐ Personal happiness
☐ Home   ☐ Other _____

Note: God does not want to take these things away from you. He just wants to be first in your life. If, as a Christian, your life focuses around any one or several of these things rather than Jesus Christ, you need to refocus your life and rearrange your priorities in order to experience God's greatest blessings.

And, if any of these things is keeping you from becoming a Christian, remember that all of these things are temporal—they will pass away. But eternal life goes on forever. Don't allow material things to keep you out of the kingdom of heaven! Accept Christ today!

FAMILY OR PERSONAL PROJECT

Discuss the practical implications of the "Life Response." What are some of the ways in which you are putting any of these things before Christ? In other words, how can you identify the problems in your own life and experience?

MOSES'
serious mistake

Have you ever made a mistake so serious that the whole world seemed to turn against you? Moses did! In fact, if he hadn't run for his life, he'd have lost it. But God didn't turn against him—nor forget him! God still had a job for him to do—in spite of his mistake.

Moses had made his decision. He had chosen to identify with his own people and their difficult plight rather than to be a part of the king's family and enjoy the earthly benefits of royalty. Somehow he knew that God destined him to deliver the children of Israel from slavery and bondage. And, once Moses made his decision, he thought he was ready to move into action.

But Moses, in spite of his great educational achievements and his ability to command armies, was not quite ready to carry out God's special plan for his life. True, he was "educated in all the learning of the Egyptians, and he was a man of power in words and deeds" (Acts 7:22). But these accomplishments did not sufficiently prepare him for the gigantic responsibility that lay before him. So, before Moses was even ready to listen to the voice of God, he had to learn that human motivation and action are not enough for so great a task. He needed a *divine* perspective as well. God's work must be done in God's way and in God's time.

Like so many of us, Moses had to make some serious mistakes to learn that lesson—a lesson he would never forget; one which would carry him through trials that would make his immediate problems appear as nothing. Little did Moses realize that he would be 40 years learning that lesson.

But we're getting ahead of the story. God knows that man often learns best through failure. Success is good and necessary, especially in early life. But when success is unbroken by failure it can lead to an over-dependence on human motivation and action. Up to this time, Moses had no doubt experienced little other than success; but he was heading now towards his first major mistake and failure.

EXODUS 2:11,12
"Now it came about in those days, when Moses had grown up, that he went out to his brethren and looked on their hard labors; and he saw an Egyptian beating a Hebrew, one of his brethren. So he looked this way and that, and when he saw

ACTS 7:23-25
"But when he was approaching the age of forty, it entered his mind to visit his brethren, the sons of Israel. And when he saw one of them being treated unjustly, he defended him and took vengeance for the oppressed by striking

there was no one around, he struck down the Egyptian and hid him in the sand."

down the Egyptian. And he supposed that his brethren understood that God was granting them deliverance through him; but they did not understand."

MOSES' INITIAL MOTIVATION

Following Moses' decision not to be identified with his Egyptian heritage, he began the process of becoming identified with his own people. And the first thing that hit him with full force, as he made his way through the field where his brethren labored as slaves, was the almost unbearable persecution that was befalling them.

Moses saw an Egyptian unmercifully beating a Hebrew, and his heart was stirred with deep feeling toward his brother. Moses wasted no time but took matters into his own hands.

MOSES' IMPETUOUS ACTION

Moses' action came in two phases—first, against the Egyptian (the problem at hand), and second, against his brethren generally.

Moses saw, no doubt in a rather secluded spot, an Egyptian taskmaster unleashing his frustration on a Hebrew slave. Moved by both compassion and anger Moses rolled up his sleeves and went into action *against the Egyptian.* The Scripture records that "he looked this way and that, and when he saw there was no one around, he struck down the Egyptian and hid him in the sand" (Exod. 2:12).

Thus Moses began, with brute strength, the process of delivering his people from Egyptian bondage. What his deeper motives were in using this physical approach, we can only speculate. No doubt Moses was in earnest about his decision to "endure ill-treatment with the people of God" and to consider "the reproach of Christ greater riches than the treasures of Egypt" (Heb. 11:25,26). But perhaps he hoped that his strong action against an overbearing Egyptian would be the evidence his brethren needed to be convinced that he was their deliverer. Perhaps he hoped the word would spread among his people: "The deliverer has come! The deliverer has come!"

But Moses was in for a rude awakening. The word spread—but not the way he might have planned! Moses did not anticipate that the children of Israel would not accept him as their deliverer. This is obvious from his next step of taking action *against his brethren.*

Stephen, in his New Testament sermon, clearly summarizes this event: "And he supposed that his brethren understood that God was granting them deliverance through him; but they did not understand. And on the following day he appeared to them as they were fighting together, and he tried to reconcile them in peace, saying, 'Men, you are brethren, why do you injure one another?' " (Acts 7:25,26).

We do not know how Moses became aware of God's specific plan for his life. Perhaps his parents shared this with him at an early age; perhaps later when he visited their little slave hut. Josephus reports that God had appeared in a dream to Amram, Moses' father, and revealed His plan for Moses to him. Even though this incident is not a part of the biblical record, it is conceivable that it happened. For God revealed Himself, through an angel, to both Zacharias and Mary and told them of the birth and destiny of both John the Baptist and Jesus Christ.

If God *did* reveal this truth to Moses' parents, it would help explain their faith and trust in God when Pharaoh issued his edict that all newborn boys be thrown into the Nile. But whatever the means God used to communicate His will to Moses, one thing is clear: at this moment, Moses was ready to fulfill God's promise to the Israelites and to take matters into his own hands and be their deliverer.

But he faced one major problem! The children of Israel didn't share Moses' vision. They did not understand that he was to be their saviour. The result was rejection!

MOSES' IMMEDIATE REJECTION

Moses' rejection also came in two phases, this time in reverse. First, he was rejected by his own people; and second, he was rejected by the Egyptians, a step that was finalized by Pharaoh himself.

EXODUS 2:13-15
"And he went out the next day, and behold, two Hebrews were fighting with each other; and he said to the offender, 'Why are you striking your companion?' But he said, 'Who made

ACTS 7:26-29
"And on the following day he appeared to them as they were fighting together, and he tried to reconcile them in peace, saying, 'Men, you are brethren, why

you a prince or a judge over us? Are you intending to kill me, as you killed the Egyptian?' Then Moses was afraid, and said, 'Surely the matter has become known.' When Pharaoh heard of this matter, he tried to kill Moses. But Moses fled from the presence of Pharaoh and settled in the land of Midian; and he sat down by a well."

do you injure one another?' But the one who was injuring his neighbor pushed him away, saying, 'Who made you ruler and judge over us? You do not mean to kill me as you killed the Egyptian yesterday, do you?' And at this remark Moses fled, and became an alien in the land of Midian, where he became the father of two sons."

The Israelites' response to Moses' intervention in their struggle must have been a shattering experience. We read: "But the one who was injuring his neighbor pushed him [Moses] away, saying, 'Who made you a ruler and judge over us?' " (Acts 7:27).

Moses was *rejected by his own people*!

Had not Moses just made one of the most sacrificial decisions that any man could make? Had he not chosen to identify with his own people and their suffering? And had he not given up the glories of Egyptian cultural splendor and position? Had he not been willing to lay his own life on the line for his brethren? After all, he had murdered an Egyptian the day before, and for *their sakes*.

And what must have hurt the most was the question that followed the rejection: "Are you intending to kill me, as you killed the Egyptian?" (Exod. 2:14). To be rejected for doing what Moses felt was right was one thing, but to be completely misunderstood was another!

When Moses heard these words of rejection from his fellow Israelite, his boldness and self-confidence immediately turned to fear. He "was afraid, and said, 'Surely the matter has become known.'"

And he had good reason to fear!

The news of his zealous activity spread like wildfire, not just among the children of Israel, but among the Egyptians as well until the news reached the king of Egypt. The news was spread by *his brethren*, the children of Israel. The ones for whom he had given up everything, the ones he felt destined to deliver, became the channel of communication back to Pharaoh! So not only was Moses rejected by his own people, but he was *rejected by all of Egypt* as well.

Moses now faced a dilemma few men ever face. He had already refused to be called the son of Pharaoh's daughter. He had given up his royal position. Even if the door had been left open for Moses to reconsider, these events burned every possible bridge. His position in Egypt was gone forever.

Nor was Moses welcome among his own people. To harbor a murderer would have brought the wrath of the king down on these poor slaves to even greater extent. Furthermore, they did not yet understand that Moses was to be their saviour. Their fear plus their lack of understanding led to Moses' total rejection.

Moses had only one choice. He had to run for his life! And run he did. Thus we read: "When Pharaoh heard of this matter, he tried to kill Moses. But Moses fled from the presence of Pharaoh and settled in the land of Midian" (Exod. 2:15).

SOME ADDITIONAL OBSERVATIONS

As we reflect back on the scriptural account (Exod. 2:11-15), there are several significant observations that stand out in bold relief: First, *Moses' motivation was primarily emotional rather than rational.*

When Moses observed the Egyptian taskmaster beating one of his brothers, he was moved with compassion—a commendable quality indeed. But at that moment his "heart" got ahead of his "head." Rather than controlling his emotions and continuing on his fact-finding mission, he lost his temper and allowed himself to get involved with a single incident. The result was an irrational act—murder—that, only one day later, got in the way of his winning the respect of his brethren.

Rational motivation is enduring; emotional motivation is up and down. Rational motivation focuses through God's perspective; emotional motivation focuses through man's perspective. God knew Moses' heart, and He also knew that the great task he had ahead of him would call for a motivational perspective that would carry him through thick and thin. Moses was not yet ready for this task. And, interestingly, although Moses later learned to be motivated from God's perspective, this weakness of losing his temper and taking matters into his own hands was to be the very thing that many years later kept him from entering the Promised Land (Num. 20:8-13).

Second, *Moses' action was primarily the result of*

39

his own strength. Moses was a strong man. No doubt on many occasions in his early life he had used this strength to his advantage. And, even after he fled Egypt and went to the land of Midian, one of his first feats was to intervene when some shepherds were harassing several women at a desert well (see Exod. 2:16-29). He drove the shepherds away, and one of the women eventually became his wife.

Physical strength, even in our own culture, is impressive. All during Moses' early life he had been admired for his physical prowess. So, at a moment when he was destined to become the deliverer he fell back upon the only thing he really knew how to use in a time of crisis, his human strength.

But God's victories usually are not won in ordinary ways. Although He often gives men supernatural ability and strength, His plan for bringing the children of Israel out of Egypt and through the wilderness called for power beyond anything Moses had ever seen or dreamed of.

Again, Moses was not ready to be their deliverer. He had yet to develop a divine perspective on being a spiritual leader. And Moses did learn that lesson. For after God had miraculously, and with *His* mighty power, delivered the children of Israel from the Egyptian army, he sang out with exultation—"Thy right hand, O Lord, is majestic in power, thy right hand, O Lord, shatters the enemy" (Exod. 15:6).

When Moses first appeared as a deliverer, he struck down an Egyptian in a moment of anger. Forty years later, God had struck down thousands. He used Moses, to be sure, but Moses knew who was the true Deliverer.

Third, in this instance, *Moses' rejection was primarily the result of his own mistakes*. Rejection, of course, is not always caused by a mistake. Consider Jesus Christ Himself who "came to His own, and those who were His own did not receive Him" (John 1:11). Moses would experience rejection again and again from the children of Israel en route from Egypt to Canaan—not because he made a lot of mistakes, but because he was doing the will of God. But this time, in Egypt, Moses' rejection by his own people and by Pharaoh was because of his own mistakes.

Moses' first mistake was that he miscalculated the response he would get from the children of Israel. Because he had grown up being the center of attention in Egypt, somehow he felt he would be "welcomed" by the people of Israel. Egocentric people generally seem to have this false perception of themselves. Moses was no exception, and he made a serious mistake. Thus, the words, "Who made *you* a prince or judge over us?" were devastating to Moses' self-image, particularly in view of his motives and sincere efforts.

Another mistake Moses made was to lose his temper and self-control and, consequently, the respect of those around him. No doubt the children of Israel who saw him kill the Egyptian also saw him look "this way and that." They also saw his fear and secretive behavior. They must have also sensed his lack of perspective on the total situation, for no man with wisdom and good sense would try to deliver the children of Israel by attacking men one by one. It would take a far greater strategy and plan to be Israel's deliverer.

Thus Moses was rejected because of unwise behavior. All of the education and experience he had received in Egypt somehow did not fully prepare him to carry out God's plan for his life. There was still much he needed to learn, and little did he know at this moment that this experience and failure was the beginning of 40 years of additional preparation for the great task God had for him.

DECISION MAKING IN THE TWENTIETH-CENTURY

No person living today can totally identify with Moses' life and ministry. His calling was unique among men and his task unequaled. Outside of Christ Himself, no man had a greater challenge calling for unusual preparation and endurance. But yet all of us can identify with certain aspects of Moses' life.

First, we've all experienced motivation that has been more *emotional* than *rational.*

And we've all experienced the short-lived results! As long as we "feel" good, we perform. When we slide off the other side of the mountain, we find ourselves in the valley and unable to carry out the goals we set for ourselves at the time we were experiencing an emotional high.

Motivation that is based on a rational approach to decision making and action is the only kind of motivation that will carry us through the vicissitudes of life. It is this kind of motivation, "ready in season and out of season" (2 Tim. 4:2), that acts when we "feel" like it and when we don't. It is this kind of motivation that enabled Jesus Christ to continue on His way to the cross, when in the garden He prayed, "My Father, if it is possible, let this cup pass from Me; yet not as I will, but as Thou wilt" (Matt. 26:39).

Too many Christians today make decisions based on emotion rather than reason. Consequently, they endure for a time—until the going gets rough—and then settle back and maintain the status quo—or less. God needs men and women who will not turn back, who will keep on carrying out the will of God no matter what the circumstances or problems in life.

Second, we've all tried to do the will of God in our own strength.

True, it does take effort, human effort, to do God's work. Yet we are not robots that operate on "supernatural batteries." So we must always remember that God's work is *God's* work, and we must never imagine we can take matters into our own hands. Paul said, "Be strong in the Lord, and in the strength of His might. Put on the full armor of God, that you may be able to stand firm against the schemes of the devil" (Eph. 6:10,11).

A careful study of this armor will show there is a unique and significant balance between human effort and reliance upon God. Man is basically responsible for having his loins girded with *truth*, for putting on the breastplate of *righteousness* and for shodding his feet with the gospel of *peace*. But it is *faith, salvation* (our position in Christ), and the *Word of God* and *prayer* that unlock the resources of heaven. Christians must always maintain this balance if they are going to be effective in God's work.

Third, all of us have experienced rejection because of our foolish mistakes.

To suffer for righteousness' sake is praiseworthy,

but to suffer because we've done something foolish is what we deserve. How easy it is to defend ourselves even when we've made a serious error! How easy it is to put the blame on someone else! If we've made a mistake we must admit it, correct the situation if we can, learn from it, and then proceed to live a more mature and responsible life.

LIFE RESPONSE

With which of these problems do you identify the most? Check that one and then think of the most recent experience that correlates with the one you've checked.

☐ Being motivated more by emotion than reason.

☐ Trying to do God's work in my own strength alone.

☐ Suffering rejection because of my own mistakes.

Think! How could you have acted differently?

Pray! Ask God to help you face life's situations in a more mature and responsible way.

Write! List what you are going to do this week to correct this problem.

FAMILY OR PERSONAL PROJECT

Discuss your "Life Response" with a close friend or with other members of your family. Pray together that God will help you to carry out your goals.

MOSES'
inferiority complex

Have you ever felt so threatened and rejected you couldn't even talk right? This was Moses' problem! In fact, his self-image was so shattered, he was afraid to respond even to God's word. Surely the Lord would give up on him now! But He didn't!

All of us can reflect back on our lives and remember negative experiences that have affected us to this day, experiences that have left their marks upon us. Some of the most common marks are feelings of inferiority and insecurity. Psychologists call these experiences *traumatic*—experiences that make a deep emotional impression.

Moses had this kind of experience. He had decided to give up the glories of Egypt to identify himself with the children of Israel. He had decided to suffer with the people of God rather than enjoy the pleasures of sin. And in the process of carrying out his sincere and sacrificial goals, he was hit broadside with rejection—

rejection from the very people he felt called to deliver from the bondage and slavery of Egypt. And this rejection led to further rejection, this time from the Egyptians, from those who had saved his life, reared him, and taught him almost everything he knew.

Moses faced a terrible dilemma. He had nowhere to turn. Consequently, he fled, a rejected and dejected man. Obviously, underneath Moses' strong, self-confident and attractive exterior was great sensitivity. He was a man so sensitive that he was affected by this rejection for the next 40 years.

GOD'S REMEMBRANCE OF ISRAEL

Moses, in his zeal to be Israel's deliverer, had taken matters into his own hands. He miscalculated God's timing. He made a serious mistake. But God did not forget Israel or Moses. He was God's man, the one the Lord had chosen to lead Israel out of Egypt. Sometimes God may appear to be deaf to our voice, but in His own time He *will* respond. (See Exod. 2:23—3:10.)

God Took Notice of Israel's Bondage

Eventually, the king of Egypt who had tried to kill Moses died. But still the slavery and persecution continued. No doubt the Pharaoh who became the new king was even more zealous in his demands on these people than his predecessors. The Scriptures tell us that the "sons of Israel *sighed* because of the bondage, and they *cried out*" (Exod. 2:23, italics added). So tragic was their plight that they groaned in utter despair.

Then God—whose timetable is often difficult for

46

human beings to comprehend—responded to their sad lament, "and their cry for help because of their bondage rose up to God ... and God remembered His covenant with Abraham, Isaac, and Jacob" (Exod. 2:23,24). God's plan for deliverance was ready to be executed, for *now* was the time for Moses to be God's human instrument to carry out that plan.

God Spoke to Moses Through a Burning Bush

For 40 years Moses had lived a quiet and reclusive shepherd's life. What a contrast from his first 40 years where he was the center of Egyptian royalty, eating at the king's table, riding in the king's chariot and commanding the king's army.

The painful experience of rejection had no doubt been forgotten. There was little reason to be afraid watching over a flock of sheep in the wilderness. Only wild animals were a serious threat, and Moses had not lost his physical strength. He could easily handle those problems.

But people are different from animals, and Moses was soon to remember how difficult people could be—how difficult to lead, how unpredictable, how fickle, how cruel! On that day when God appeared to Moses in the burning bush and issued a call to be Israel's deliverer, old memories quickly surfaced. Old emotional wounds were torn open. Old fears gripped Moses' total being. He immediately began to offer excuses to God. His resistance was quick and defensive. But God's time was *now*, and His communication with Moses was persistent. Moses could not escape. God's hand was heavy upon him. (See Exod. 3:1-10.)

MOSES' RESISTANCE AND GOD'S RESPONSE

First, let's get an overall perspective of the dialogue between God and Moses. (See Exod. 3:11—4:12.)

RESISTANCE	RESPONSE
Moses: "Who am I?" (3:11)	*God*: "I will be with you." (3:12)
Moses: "What shall I say to them?" (3:13)	*God*: "Say to the sons of Israel, 'I AM has sent me to you.'" (3:14)
Moses: "What if they will not believe me, or listen to what I say?" (4:1)	*God*: He gave Moses three signs—the rod that would become a serpent, the leprous hand, and the water that would turn to blood. (4:2-9)
Moses: "I have never been eloquent . . . . I am slow of speech and slow of tongue." (4:10)	*God*: "I will be with your mouth, and teach you what you are to say." (4:12)

Now let's look more closely at Moses' problem. *Why* did he resist God's call? *Why* did he make up these excuses? What was at the root of his problem?

Moses' First Excuse

"Who am I?" (3:11). What a contrast! Forty years before, Moses was so *self-confident* he had tried to deliver the children of Israel in his own strength. Now he felt so inferior and worthless that he believed himself totally incapable of so great a task.

48

Moses' perspective had changed. Forty years before he had looked at the job from the viewpoint of a successful general, one who had masterfully led the Egyptian army in victory over the Ethiopians. "Why not? Look *who I am*!" implied Moses.

But *now*, 40 years later, he saw the task from the viewpoint of a lowly shepherd. Life had no doubt been relatively easy for Moses. Sheep are not known for rejecting the shepherd. And wild animals that attack (compared with human enemies) are relatively easy to outsmart and drive away.

But when Moses said, "Who am I?" he was reflecting more than a desire to escape from responsibility. And he was reflecting more than humility. He was reflecting an attitude of worthlessness and inferiority —an unusual and abnormal lack of self-confidence. Moses was still suffering from the rejection he had experienced so many years before.

And note! Moses wasn't remembering a traumatic experience in childhood. Moses had been a *grown man* when he was rejected by Egyptians and Israelites alike. Emotional rejection can hit at any age and can affect us deeply, no matter how secure our early years.

God's response was sympathetic, but direct. "Certainly I will be with you" (3:12). Moses had not yet learned *why* he had failed in his first mission. He knew little of God's approach in solving problems. He had moved into action primarily because of his own motivation, experience and training. He knew little of God's power and leadership in his life.

God understood Moses' problem! This is one reason why He appeared in a burning bush. True, this

49

was an unusual way to get his attention, to get him to listen. But it was also a very dramatic way to let Moses in on a very important truth—*God can do anything*!

For the average man, a dramatic and direct word from God would be enough to get response. But Moses, at this point, was not average. His emotional problem was so deep he resisted even further!

Moses' Second Excuse

"What shall I say to them when they ask your name?" (3:13, paraphrase).

Though Moses was suffering from deep emotional rejection, he had learned a valuable lesson—one that would aid him the rest of his life. He had learned that he needed an *authority* beyond himself. Though the name "Moses" was once great in Egypt, and perhaps even among the children of Israel, it had not been sufficient to convince others he was the deliverer.

God's response to Moses' question was almost as dramatic as the burning bush: "Thus you shall say to the sons of Israel, 'I AM has sent me to you'" (3:14). God contrasted Himself with the *many* gods of Egypt. He is the *one true God*! In reality there are no other "gods."

Also, God is the eternally existing One, ever present to help His people. In a small way, in a human way, God had already revealed this to Moses when He spoke from the burning bush:

"I AM the God of Abraham, the God of Isaac, and the God of Jacob." In other words, I AM the covenantal God of the PAST! (3:6)

"I have surely seen the affliction of My people who

are in Egypt." In other words, I AM the compassionate God of the PRESENT! (3:7)

"I have come down to deliver them . . . and to bring them up from that land to a good and spacious land, to a land flowing with milk and honey." In other words, I AM the consummating God of the FUTURE! (3:8)

God had illustrated His "I AM-ness" in words Moses could grasp! Eternal existence is difficult to comprehend, but history is understandable. It is within space and time. But now Moses was ready for an additional insight into God's personality, and so He said, in response to Moses' question, "Thus you shall say to the sons of Israel, 'The Lord, the God of your fathers, the God of Abraham, the God of Isaac, and the God of Jacob, has sent me to you.' *This is My name forever*" (3:15).

Moses' Third Excuse

"What if they will not believe me, or listen to what I say?" (4:1).

Even if Moses was convinced of God's power and greatness, and I think he was, he was still unconvinced he could persuade the children of Israel that God had sent him. And with this third excuse, we can get a much clearer glimpse of the root of Moses' problem. Forty years before, Moses had presented himself to the people assuming that they would understand that "God was granting them deliverance through him" (Acts 7:25). They had responded with rejection: "Who made you a prince or a judge over us?" (Exod. 2:14).

Moses still remembered the stinging words and

forceful hand that had "pushed him away" (Acts 7: 27). He knew by direct experience the emotional rejection. After 40 years, feelings of fear that had long been repressed and forgotten suddenly surfaced and overwhelmed him.

Again God understood. He told Moses He would help him. He would enable him, as it were, to transport the "burning bush" to Egypt to perform three dramatic and authenticating miracles in order to convince the children of Israel that God had really sent him. First, he would be able to turn the shepherd's staff into a serpent and again into a staff. Second, he could cause his own hand to become leprous and whole again. And third, he would be able to pour water from the sacred Nile on the ground and turn it into blood (see Exod. 4:2-9).

Moses' Fourth Excuse

"I have never been eloquent .... I am slow of speech and slow of tongue" (4:10).

Moses' final excuse is almost humorous, yet pathetic. It is a statement mixed with rationalizations and reality. To state that he had "never been eloquent" was to *deny* reality, for Stephen gave us a true perspective of Moses' ability as a young man in Egypt —"he was a man of *power in words* and deeds" (Acts 7:22).

At one time Moses had been *very* eloquent. Somehow Moses had forgotten and even dared to rationalize his problem before God. But Moses was no doubt also "telling it as it was." Though at one time he *had* been able to communicate fluently and to use words dramatically, he now had "lost his touch," his ability.

He was "slow of speech and slow of tongue."

Humanly speaking, why would this be true? First, Moses had long since left the environment of Egypt that was permeated with educational opportunities. There he had had constant exposure to the latest information and knowledge, regular opportunities to learn by experience, and regular dialogue with fellow Egyptians who were some of the greatest scholars in the world. But for 40 years Moses had been away from these stimuli with little opportunity to demonstrate skills he had once so capably used. It is only logical to conclude that the many years he had spent alone on the back side of the desert, shepherding a flock of sheep, was not the most conducive atmosphere in which to maintain his speaking ability.

But there is another reason, perhaps more important, for Moses' problem. With the rejection and loss of self-confidence may have come an incompetence, an inability to do what he once could do with great fervor and excellence. Feelings of inferiority and insecurity can have a dramatic effect on a man's ability to communicate effectively. Moses was no doubt suffering from this effect.

Again, God, in His love, was sympathetic to Moses' problem. He said in response: "I . . . will be with your mouth, and teach you what you are to say" (4:12).

But Moses was still not ready or willing to obey God. And Moses' final response tried God's patience.

MOSES' RELUCTANT OBEDIENCE

Moses finally gave in, reluctantly. Furthermore, he

wanted someone to go with him to speak for him and to assist him in doing what God wanted *him* to do alone (Exod. 4:13).

God's sympathetic understanding towards Moses' problem suddenly turned to anger (4:14). God had done every logical thing to help Moses overcome his handicap. But in His willingness to cooperate with men's weaknesses, God took one more step. He approved an alternate plan. This plan would allow Aaron, Moses' brother, to assist him as he went back to Egypt to face the children of Israel and eventually the king himself (4:14—5:1). Ultimately, as we will see, Moses' reluctance to do the job God had called him to do alone, proved to be as much a burden for Moses as a blessing. In the end, God's perfect will is *always* better than His permissive will.

LESSONS FOR TWENTIETH-CENTURY LIVING

There are several significant lessons we can learn from this passage. And probably most of us can identify with all of them.

First, Moses was a human being just like you and me. And yet God used him in spite of his weaknesses. I'm glad for this lesson, aren't you? There is hope for everyone of us. In spite of our shortcomings, our failures, our weaknesses, God *can* use us.

Second, Moses needed to arrive at a balance in his life between "self-confidence" and "God-confidence." He went to two extremes. First he said, "I can do it!" Then he said, "I can't do it!" For the Christian, both are true when stated properly. As Paul said, "*I* can do all things through *Him* who strengthens *me*" (Phil. 4:13).

54

Third, Moses was a sensitive person. And sensitive people can be affected most by negative experiences. Moses felt very keenly the effects of rejection, even as a grown man who had a secure background. He developed a personality problem that interfered with God's plan for his life. And his major problem, of course, was that he began to use his problem as an excuse for not doing God's will.

All of us can identify with this problem. All of us have weaknesses in our personalities that cause us to draw back, to refuse to act responsibly and to do what we know we *must* do. Our tendency is to *rationalize* our behavior, just like Moses, and even to fail in taking advantage of the opportunities God gives us to overcome our problems.

Fourth, and perhaps most important, Moses failed to see what God was attempting to accomplish in his life, in spite of his personal failure. God was taking a bad experience, one of Moses' own making, and was using it to equip him for his future ministry.

You see, God knew what lay ahead for Moses. He knew that Moses' rejection in Egypt 40 years before would fade into "nothingness" in relationship to the rejection he would face in the future as he began carrying out God's will and leading the children of Israel out of Egypt. The very thing that caused Moses to almost miss God's will would enable him to handle the even greater problems that lay ahead. This will become abundantly clear in future chapters on Moses' life and leadership.

All of us have faced problems that we do not understand. It would not be right to blame God for structuring these circumstances, for frequently they are caused by sins of others, and at other times they are of our own doing. The important point is that God can take a bad experience, no matter *who* caused it, and turn it into a blessing—that is, if we see things from God's perspective.

And what is God's perspective? Paul stated it succinctly: "And we know that God causes all things to work together for good to those who love God, to those who are called according to His purpose" (Rom. 8:28).

LIFE RESPONSE

With which of Moses' problems do you identify most? Check one:

☐ 1. An inability for Moses to see how God could use him—*with* all of his weaknesses and failures.

☐ 2. Moses' problem of balance between "self-confidence" and "God (Christ) confidence."

☐ 3. Moses' inferiority complex.

☐ 4. Moses' inability to see how God was using present failures to equip him for future service.

What one specific step that you have never taken before, can you take now to overcome this problem? Write down *what* you are going to do and *when* you are going to do it.

FAMILY OR PERSONAL PROJECT

Review this message and then discuss your life response with someone you trust. Seek their prayer support and suggestions for overcoming your specific problem.

MOSeS'
self-image rebuilt

Did you know that God is more concerned about your self-image than you are? Moses learned that lesson! Perhaps you need to learn it, too.

Yes, Moses had a problem! He had suffered severe emotional disturbance when he was rejected, first by his own people and then by the Egyptians. He had lost his confidence. And 40 years in a foreign land, enjoying the quiet life of a shepherd had not helped to rebuild his self-image. In fact, it seems he rather enjoyed this life with its few demands and threats.

But Moses was a "marked" man. God had plans for him—plans that would call for unusual self-confidence blended with a proper perspective of God's power. But Moses was not yet ready emotionally. When God called to him from the burning bush, he offered several rather understandable excuses. And God *did* understand. He patiently, but directly, began to help Moses develop a proper perspective of the great task He had for him, the task of leading the children of Israel out of Egypt, through the wilderness and into the Promised Land.

But you'll remember that Moses finally acquiesced to God's call—not because of a restored self-image—but because of God's gentle, but persistent demand that he do so. In fact, God finally became impatient with Moses and consented to Aaron, Moses' brother, accompanying him to Egypt and assisting him in communicating with the children of Israel and with Pharaoh.

But God was not through with Moses. As we'll see, His compromise in allowing Aaron to help Moses was only temporary. God still wanted *Moses* to be able to handle the leadership of Israel with a blend of proper self-confidence and strong faith in His power. Exodus 5—14 is an intriguing account of how God, through a rather natural process, rebuilt Moses' self-image.

It is easy to miss this process. The miracles and plagues that God brought on the Egyptians are so overwhelming and outstanding that they overshadow Moses the man. But Moses the man is there, nonetheless, and God was not only demonstrating His great power to Israel, the Egyptians, and the whole world, but He was working in the life of a man He loved, restoring his self-confidence and preparing him for one of the greatest tasks ever faced by a human being.

Let's look at that process!

SOME INITIAL TESTS

Before Moses was ready for the main process of

confronting Pharaoh and being God's channel to unleash God's power and fury upon an unbelieving and pagan people, he needed some initial tests that would strike directly at the heart of Moses' problem—an inferiority complex brought on by rejection. Notice how precisely these events zero in on Moses' weakness. (See Exod. 4:27—7:14.)

The First Test

When Moses returned to Egypt with Aaron, he and his brother did as God had commanded (4:27, 28). They "assembled all the elders of the sons of Israel; and Aaron spoke all the words which the Lord had spoken to Moses. He then performed the signs in the sight of the people" (4:29,30).

The result must have been very gratifying. The "people believed" what Moses and Aaron had to say. "They bowed low and worshiped" (4:31). What a welcome contrast this must have been for Moses in comparison with his rejection experience 40 years earlier.

But the test was just beginning. In fact, Moses probably didn't even see the significance of what was about to happen until much later. You see, Pharaoh was not as easy to convince. Rather, he rejected outright the message Moses and Aaron brought to him. He even put a greater burden on the children of Israel, insisting on the same production level without providing the necessary materials to make bricks. The children of Israel not only had to maintain the same quota of bricks, but also gather the materials to make them. (See Exod. 5:1-18.)

Predictably, their reactions were immediate and

extreme. Israel's attitude was anything but sympathetic. They turned against Moses and Aaron. And their words were strong and bitter—"May the Lord look upon you and judge you, for you have made us odious in Pharoah's sight and in the sight of his servants, to put a sword in their hand to kill us" (5:21).

What a reversal! And imagine what must have happened to Moses. What bitter memories must have surfaced! What a strong urge must have flooded his being—an urge to hide, to run, to once again escape to a foreign land and become a quiet and gentle shepherd, free from the pressure and tension of this awesome leadership responsibility.

He *did* run! But this time in the right direction—straight to the Lord. "O, Lord!" he cried. "Why hast Thou brought harm to this people? Why didst Thou ever send me? Ever since I came to Pharaoh to speak in Thy name, he has done harm to this people; and Thou hast not delivered Thy people at all" (5:22,23).

True, Moses was disillusioned and confused. He also lacked faith. In fact, he even forgot what God had told him from the burning bush—that upon his initial encounter, Pharaoh *would not* allow the children of Israel to leave Egypt (Exod. 3:19,20). In other words, Moses should not have been surprised at Pharaoh's reaction.

But now, all Moses could remember was the rejection, the pain and frustration he had felt before. Still, he *was making progress*. Rather than trying to escape, like a Jonah headed for Ninevah, he turned to the Lord. He poured out his anxiety to the only one who could answer his questions. And for Moses, that was significant progress.

The Second Test

Again, God's response to Moses' frustration was sympathetic. He reiterated for Moses His plan, His definite intention to deliver the children of Israel from Egyptian bondage (Exod. 6:1-5). But with this sympathetic response came another painful directive to Moses: "Say, therefore, to the sons of Israel, 'I am the Lord, and I will bring you out from under the burdens of the Egyptians, and I will deliver you from their bondage. I will also redeem you with an outstretched arm and with great judgments' " (6:6).

Moses obeyed. But he no doubt did so with fear and anxiety and ambivalence. And lo and behold, the results were negative. The children of Israel "did not listen to Moses on account of their despondency and cruel bondage" (6:9).

Again, rejection!

Moses must have felt that God's next directive was the final blow: "Go, tell Pharaoh king of Egypt to let the sons of Israel go out of his land" (6:11). And understandably, it must have been very painful—so painful that Moses regressed to his final excuse he offered God that day when He had spoken to him from the burning bush: "Behold, the sons of Israel have not listened to me; how then will Pharaoh listen to me, for I am *unskilled in speech?*" (6:12).

The Third Test

Interestingly, God's response to Moses' regression was very similar to His response to Moses' excuses in the wilderness. Again, God did not condemn Moses! He just kept Moses moving in the direction of doing His will (Exod. 7:1-13).

Moses' staff was to be the catalyst. He was to take it and throw it down before Pharaoh, and it would "become a serpent" (7:9). Moses' response seemed to be instantaneous. His rebound was quick. He obeyed God, reflecting great progress in developing self-confidence, and most of all, learning to trust God.

The results, of course, had already been predicted. Pharaoh rejected the miracle. But now Moses was ready to move on to the main process that God would use to make Pharaoh let His people go—a process that would also put the finishing touches on Moses' emotional and spiritual rehabilitation.

THE MAIN PROCESS OF REHABILITATION

Through Moses and Aaron, God allowed ten supernatural and awesome plagues to come upon Egypt in order to convince Pharaoh that he should set the children of Israel free from slavery. (See Exod. 7:14—12:37.) And, as is often true, a single act of God can have several purposes. God's *primary purpose* in these plagues was to convince Israel, the Egyptians, and the whole world that He was the one true God! (Exod. 9:16; Rom. 9:17). Moses and Aaron were having a part in carrying out the "great commission" in the Old Testament. But as already explained, God was also carrying out a *secondary purpose* within this process: He was rebuilding Moses' self-confidence.

Beyond doubt, the following scriptural statements illustrate this secondary purpose. As you read, notice the transition. Aaron, as a prominent figure in the process of communication between God and Pharaoh, began to phase out and Moses became the predominant figure. In fact, by the end of the third plague, God was already speaking directly to Pharaoh through Moses. And Moses, rather than Aaron, was directly involved in performing the miracles. God had finally brought His servant to the place where he was carrying out the task He had originally called him to do, and almost totally without Aaron's assistance.

Following are statements under each plague that clearly show this pattern (italics added):

The Plague of Water to Blood
7:14—"Then the Lord said to *MOSES*"
7:19—"Then the Lord said to *MOSES*, 'Say to *Aaron*'"
7:20—"So *MOSES* and *Aaron* did even as the Lord had commanded."

The Plague of Frogs
8:1—"Then the Lord said to *MOSES*"
8:5—"Then the Lord said to *MOSES*, 'Say to *Aaron*'"
8:9—"And *MOSES* said to Pharaoh"

The Plague of Gnats
8:16—"Then the Lord said to *MOSES*, 'Say to *Aaron*'"
8:17—"And *Aaron* stretched out his hand."

The Plague of Insects
8:20—"Now the Lord said to *MOSES*"
8:26—"But *MOSES* said"
8:29—"Then *MOSES* said"

8:30—"So *MOSES* went out."

The Plague of Pestilence
9:1—"Then the Lord said to *MOSES*"

The Plague of Boils
9:8—"Then the Lord said to *MOSES* and *Aaron*,
    'Take for yourselves handfuls of soot from a
    kiln, and let *MOSES* throw it toward the
    sky in the sight of Pharaoh.' "
9:10—"And *MOSES* threw it toward the sky."

The Plague of Hail
9:13—"Then the Lord said to *MOSES*"
9:22—"Now the Lord said to *MOSES*"
9:23—"And *MOSES* stretched out his staff."

The Plague of Locusts
10:1—"Then the Lord said to *MOSES*"
10:3—"And *MOSES* and *Aaron* ... said to
    Pharaoh"
10:12—"Then the Lord said to *MOSES*"
10:13—"So *MOSES* stretched out his staff over
    the land of Egypt."

The Plague of Darkness
10:21—"Then the Lord said to *MOSES*"
10:22—"So *MOSES* stretched out his hand toward
    the sky."

The Plague of Death
11:1—"Now the Lord said to *MOSES*"
11:4—"And *MOSES* said, 'Thus says the Lord.' "

THE FINAL RESULTS—
SELF-CONFIDENCE AND GOD-CONFIDENCE

The basic result of the process God took Moses through was a greater degree of self-esteem. And correlated closely with this self-esteem was an ability to trust and obey God. And a further correlation is seen in that Moses' self-esteem was also directly related to how well he was respected and accepted in Egypt. In fact, by the end of the ninth plague, we are told that Moses "was greatly esteemed in the land of Egypt, both in the sight of Pharaoh's servants and in the sight of the people" (Exod. 11:3).

Social acceptance and self-confidence, then, were directly correlated with Moses' ability to trust and obey God, to feel comfortable in carrying out God's will. This is clear from the process God took Moses through. (See Exod. 11:4—13:22.) Little by little He rebuilt Moses' self-image until he was able to handle murmuring and criticism with an unusual amount of confidence and trust in God.

The greatest evidence of this truth is very clear from Moses' reaction when the Egyptians were pursuing the children of Israel. The Red Sea was in front of them, and the Egyptian army was coming up fast behind them. Humanly speaking, there was no way to escape (14:1-10).

Terror overtook the Israelites. Then, anger. And against whom? Moses, of course! And this was one of the moments God had been preparing Moses to face.

A year earlier he would have no doubt crumbled under the pressure. But not now. This was one test he wouldn't fail. And at this point we can see the pattern

—failure in small tests can sometimes prepare us to pass the big one! And Moses passed with flying colors.

Listen to the complaints from the children of Israel: "Then they said to Moses, 'Is it because there were no graves in Egypt that you have taken us away to die in the wilderness? Why have you dealt with us in this way, bringing us out of Egypt? Is this not the word that we spoke to you in Egypt, saying, "Leave us alone that we may serve the Egyptians"? For it would have been better for us to serve the Egyptians than to die in the wilderness' " (14:11,12).

And now listen to Moses' instant response, reflecting both self-confidence and trust in Jehovah: "But Moses said to the people, 'Do not fear! Stand by and see the salvation of the Lord which He will accomplish for you today; for the Egyptians whom you have seen today, you will never see them again forever. The Lord will fight for you while you keep silent' " (14:13,14).

And the Lord did fight for Israel. Moses stretched out his staff, that marvelous symbol of God's power, and the sea was divided. The children of Israel marched across on dry ground. And once on the other side, Moses stretched out his staff again, causing the powerful waters to rush in on the Egyptians, drowning horses and riders. (See Exod. 14:15-28.)

Israel was safe on the other side. They were free from Egyptian bondage at last (14:29,30). And when they "saw the great power which the Lord had used against the Egyptians, the people feared the Lord, and they believed in the Lord and in His servant Moses" (14:31).

PSYCHOLOGICAL PROBLEMS
AND THE TWENTIETH-CENTURY CHRISTIAN

1. Today some Christians believe that conversion automatically solves all psychological problems. But emotional healing is usually a process that takes time. Even when God was performing unbelievable miracles in Egypt, He still used a natural process to restore Moses' public image, his self-confidence and his proper perspective of God Himself.

2. God is interested in every problem we face. And He is particularly concerned that emotional problems such as insecurity, inferiority feelings, and anxiety do not stand in our way of trusting and obeying Him. He wants us to enjoy His will. In other words, He does not want emotional problems to hold us back spiritually.

3. In the process of overcoming emotional problems, it sometimes gets worse before it gets better. This was true of Moses. It was painful to face God's call and to fail some of the initial tests. But it was necessary to *begin* acting responsibly before he could begin to *enjoy* acting responsibly.

4. It is easy to regress to earlier patterns of behavior, to experience old fears and anxieties. Moses did! And so will we. But if we are making steady progress, an ability to rebound will become easier and quicker.

5. Acceptance by others is basic to self-acceptance and self-confidence; and self-confidence and acceptance are basic to being able to trust and obey God, to have confidence in God and to walk by faith. This brings into focus the importance of the intimate relationships that should be fostered in a Christian family as well as in the Body of Christ. God uses fathers,

mothers, brothers and sisters, and members of the Body of Christ to meet the emotional and social needs of people. True and vital Christianity is relational, and relational Christianity is necessary to produce mature Christian personalities.

6. God is patient with our emotional problems. He is very understanding, as He was with Moses. But He will not tolerate consistent irresponsible behavior, especially when He provides us with opportunities to overcome our problems. We are asking for trouble if we constantly ignore God's help in these areas of our lives. Probably the most serious result will be that eventually God will just allow us to go on in our self-pity and insecurity and other problems.

7. When working to overcome problems of insecurity, we may need a temporary "crutch" to help us develop our self-confidence. Moses needed an Aaron, and God provided him with one. But remember! God's preference was that Moses depend primarily on Him—not on Aaron.

8. When supporting and helping others with problems of insecurity, withdraw your support gradually and sensitively, as God did with Moses. Always have as your goal the development of mature and independent personalities in others.

9. No matter what our maturity, we are always vulnerable, particularly in the areas where we once were weak. And of course, we're always vulnerable in areas where we're strong. Both situations were true of Moses. In his early life his greatest strength was security, which became his vulnerable area. Later in his life his greatest weakness was insecurity, which continued to be an area of vulnerability. As we'll see in

future chapters, Moses had trouble maintaining a balance in his weak areas. And so, we too must always be on guard.

10. And finally (and perhaps most important for many people) we are never too old to start developing our self-confidence. Remember! Moses was 80! How old are you?

LIFE RESPONSE

Select one person, Christian or non-Christian, who is having a problem with insecurity and inferiority. Perhaps it is one of your children, or your husband or your wife. What can you do to tactfully help that person develop his or her self-confidence?

And remember, if someone tries to help you, don't be too proud to accept the help! And also remember, in helping others, you help yourself.

FAMILY OR PERSONAL PROJECT

Discuss this chapter with your family or with some close Christian friends. Then zero in on the twentieth-century application. Use each point as a basis for discussion. What points are particularly applicable to your life?

MOSES' SONG
a true test of maturity

Have you ever been tempted to take credit for something you didn't do? People with self-image problems often do, you know. Moses faced this moment, too, but particularly on one occasion.

What a contrast! In the wilderness by a burning bush in conversation with God, Moses had resisted the Lord's call! "I can't do it!" he cried. "I'm not capable!"

A year or so later, back in Egypt, with the Red Sea before him and the Egyptian army coming up behind, Moses cried out to the children of Israel, "Do not fear! Stand by and see the salvation of the Lord which He will accomplish for you today!"

There is only one conclusion from the facts. Moses had come a *long, long* way—from a man who was so insecure he couldn't speak properly, to a man whose self-image had been completely restored. And not

70

only had Moses become *psychologically* mature, but he had also become *spiritually* mature. He had learned to trust and honor God, to give Him first place in his life. Moses' song, recorded in Exodus 15:1-21, clearly illustrates this truth.

MOSES' SONG OF VICTORY

Moses "was educated in all the learning of the Egyptians," which obviously included the arts. His ability to compose both graphic poetry and meaningful music is clearly evident in the song he wrote following Israel's great victory over Egypt.

The song has a single theme, which seemingly was also the chorus. It is stated twice: "I will sing to the Lord, for He is highly exalted; the horse and its rider He has hurled into the sea" (15:1,21).

The thrust of this theme is very clear. The Lord had been greatly exalted and honored through this significant event. Consequently, the children of Israel were raising their voices in a song of praise and adoration. The event, of course, was the Egyptian defeat, and it is succinctly summarized in the second line: "The horse and its rider He has hurled into the sea."

We cannot say for sure how this song was actually presented and performed, but it seems that after each stanza, the women of Israel, led by Moses' sister Miriam, broke forth with dancing and singing, repeating this theme chorus (15:20,21).

Moses developed this theme further with three stanzas. Each stanza, in turn, has a sub-theme. Each sub-theme is followed by a detailed description of how God had won this great victory over Egypt, hurling the "horse and its rider . . . into the sea."

The First Stanza

THE SUB-THEME:

"The Lord is my strength and song,
And He has become my salvation;
This is my God, and I will praise Him;
My father's God, and I will extol Him" (15:2).

THE SUB-THEME PARAPHRASED:

They were delivered by God's strength and power.

THE DETAILED DESCRIPTION:

"The Lord is a warrior;
The Lord is His name.
Pharaoh's chariots and his army He has cast into
  the sea;
And the choicest of his officers are drowned in the
  Red Sea.
The deeps cover them;
They went down into the depths like a stone"
  (15:3-5).

The Second Stanza

THE SUB-THEME:

"Thy right hand, O Lord, is majestic in power,
Thy right hand, O Lord, shatters the enemy"
  (15:6).

THE SUB-THEME PARAPHRASED:

God's righteous anger is eventually unleashed
  against those who continually resist Him and
  fight against Him.

THE DETAILED DESCRIPTION:

"And in the greatness of Thine excellence Thou
  dost overthrow those who rise up against Thee;
Thou dost send forth They burning anger, and it
  consumes them as chaff.

And at the blast of Thy nostrils the waters were
    piled up,
The flowing waters stood up like a heap;
The deeps were congealed in the heart of the sea.
The enemy said, 'I will pursue, I will overtake, I
    will divide the spoil;
My desire shall be gratified against them;
I will draw out my sword, my hand shall destroy
    them.'
Thou didst blow with Thy wind, the sea covered
    them; they sank like lead in the mighty waters"
    (15:7-10).

The Third Stanza
THE SUB-THEME:
"Who is like Thee among the gods, O Lord?
Who is like Thee, majestic in holiness,
Awesome in praises, working wonders?" (15:11).
THE SUB-THEME PARAPHRASED:
God is the one true and eternal God, the only one
    who is holy, to be feared, and who is able to work
    great miracles.
THE DETAILED DESCRIPTION:
"Thou didst stretch out Thy right hand,
The earth swallowed them.
In Thy lovingkindness Thou hast led the people
    whom Thou hast redeemed;
In Thy strength Thou hast guided them to Thy
    holy habitation.
The peoples have heard, they tremble;
Anguish has gripped the inhabitants of Philistia.
Then the chiefs of Edom were dismayed;
The leaders of Moab, trembling grips them;

All the inhabitants of Canaan have melted away.
Terror and dread fall upon them;
By the greatness of Thine arm they are motionless
as stone;
Until Thy people pass over, O Lord,
Until the people pass over whom Thou hast pur-
chased.
Thou wilt bring them and plant them in the moun-
tain of Thine inheritance,
The place, O Lord, which Thou hast made for Thy
dwelling,
The sanctuary, O Lord, which Thy hands have
established.
The Lord shall reign forever and ever" (15:12-18).

REFLECTIONS OF MATURITY

In the previous chapter, we saw how easy it is to miss Moses' development during the plagues because of their sensational nature. Just so, we could easily miss one of the greatest lessons in this song of victory, that is, how its content is a measure of the man, Moses.

Let's reconstruct the context! Remember, Moses had experienced tremendous growth spiritually and psychologically. He had moved from a position of fear and almost total dependence on his brother Aaron to the place where he alone became God's spokesman and human instrument in performing miracles. It was Moses, the once timid shepherd, who with fantastic confidence and faith in God stretched out his staff over the Red Sea and parted the waters. And when on the other side, it was he who once again stretched out his staff and caused the waters to come crushing in on the Egyptian army. It was this same Moses who sat down with heartfelt adoration and praise to God and penned this song of victory. And in doing so, Moses let us in on what had happened to him personally. In this song are some outstanding reflections of spiritual and psychological maturity.

Moses Had a Proper Perspective of Himself in Relationship to God

Was it not Moses, the man, who had stretched out his hand, precipitating the plague of insects? Had he not thrown the soot into the sky, bringing the plague of boils? Did not the lightning begin to flash, the thunder roar and the hail begin to fall when Moses stretched out *his* staff? And who was it but Moses that pronounced the plague of death that smote the firstborn in all of Egypt? And as we've seen, that great climactic miracle of the Red Sea was wrought at the hand of Moses!

But where is Moses' name in the song of victory? Obviously, it does not appear—and for good reason —Moses had learned that man is but an instrument in God's hands, an instrument that can only function with God's permission and assistance.

Thus, this song is to the Lord and about the Lord, and about what He had done for Israel. Thus, in the *New American Standard Bible*, the name of the Lord God of Israel appears 13 times in the song. In addition, there are 33 pronouns (Him, He, Thine, Thou, Thee, etc.)—a total of 46 references to the name of the Lord.

This song then reflects Moses' mature perspective of himself in relationship to God. Some 40 years before, he had tried to deliver Israel with his own "right hand" striking down an Egyptian taskmaster. He had set out to be the deliverer—in his *own* strength. And now 40 years later, Moses set the record straight when he said, *"Thy right hand*, O Lord, is majestic in power, *Thy right hand*, O Lord, shatters the enemy" (15:6).

Yes, God used Moses' mouth, his abilities, his personality—and even his "right arm." And now Moses knew who really made it all possible.

Moses Had a Proper Perspective of Himself in Relationship to the Children of Israel

Moses' maturity was not only theological, but also practical. His statements in the song about God as the deliverer were not just pious phrases, but words of action. They were reflective of his life-style, not just his verbalizations.

Put another way, Moses could now handle success as well as failure. This is a true mark of maturity. If Moses had succeeded too soon as the great leader of Israel, particularly in his early years of life, he would no doubt have been carried away with pride and self-glorification. But he had been prepared for this moment of glory and prestige, a moment he could handle with true humility. He had learned his lesson. Forty years before, his attitudes of superiority had been shattered. The slow but steady process of rebuilding his self-image had brought Moses to the place of true perspective of both his relationship with God and man.

Moses' maturity at this moment can no doubt best be seen by the fact that he perceived all too well that

Israel would be tempted to glorify him, to perhaps even make him their god-king. The Scriptures are very clear that following the Red Sea adventure, the people not only "believed in the Lord," but also "in His servant Moses." And remember, too, that Israel was yet carnal, very carnal. After years of exposure to pagan gods and a worldly life-style, they were far from ready to respond maturely to so great a deliverance.

It does not take a great imagination to see the great moment of opportunism that was at Moses' disposal at this moment in his life. Had he been immature and selfish, this would have been his opportunity to become a great man in the eyes of men, not only among the children of Israel, but among the pagan nations as well. After all, it was Moses who had spoken, who had held out his hand, who had held out his staff for all to hear and see.

But the picture is clear. Moses guarded against this misinterpretation by writing a song that reflected the truth. If Israel took the words seriously, which I believe they did, there would be no way for them to focus their eyes on Moses rather than God. True, Moses was involved, and they believed in him, but now they saw him in proper perspective.

Moses' message, then, to Israel and to the world, is crystal clear. It was the one and only Lord God who had delivered Israel from Egypt. Moses was merely a human instrument who had cooperated with God—and hesitantly at that. And in view of the attempts Moses made to escape from this awesome task, there is no way a thinking man could have doubted the fact that *God* did it, and not Moses.

PERSONAL ACHIEVEMENTS
AND THE TWENTIETH-CENTURY CHRISTIAN

Twentieth-century man has—and always will have —a problem *maintaining a proper view of himself in relationship to God.* In fact, twentieth-century man has pretty much forgotten God. True, we have accomplished great things in this century. We have discovered nuclear power and how to harness that power. We've made great advances in medical science, discovering fantastic vaccines and developing almost unbelievable surgical skills. We have conquered many natural laws—developing radio, television, jet power and missile systems. We've even put man on the moon and brought him safely back to earth.

Ask the average man what *man* has accomplished and he'll tell you. Pick up the average history or science book and you'll discover what man thinks of himself. Look for the name of God, and you may look in vain. Generally speaking, man does not acknowledge God's role in his accomplishments. Rather, he acknowledges himself.

Twentieth-century man has also had a problem *maintaining a proper perspective of himself in relationship to his fellow man.* In fact, part of his strategy is to use every opportunity for self-promotion, to advance himself, to win the applause of others. And if he can't *win* their admiration, he'll demand it when the opportunity presents itself. Man by nature is an opportunist. He has one great concern—himself.

What about the Christian? What about you? Have you developed a proper perspective—both in your relationship to God and to others? Remember! Only a mature Christian can have a true perspective. On the one hand, he knows that God uses men: their ability, their self-confidence, their personalities. He has no difficulty accepting his worth and his need for self-esteem. He also knows he needs to be appreciated and he needs to show appreciation towards others. He knows he needs recognition and he needs to achieve and feel successful.

But on the other hand, he knows that without God, he would be nothing at all. He knows his very life and breath are from God. And when it comes to evaluating his achievements, he is quick to honor and glorify God, his Creator and His Saviour. And furthermore, when he is in a position where he could easily manipulate people for self-glorification, he is quick to evaluate his motives and to take specific steps to direct man's attention to the One who alone is worthy of man's praise. He practices on earth what someday he'll practice in heaven as represented by the 24 elders in the book of Revelation (Rev. 4:10, 11).

LIFE RESPONSE
Use the following questions to help you evaluate your perspective:

1. How often do I use the little words "I" and "me" in my conversations with myself and with others?

2. On the other hand, am I characterized by "false humility"—trying to give the impression I am honoring God and others, but merely camouflaging my motives and actions with words?

3. How often do I use the words "thank you" when talking to God and others?

4. How often is God in my thoughts, compared with thoughts about myself?

5. How well am I able to handle "success" as well as "failure"?

Note: People who have a weak self-image often have the most difficult time handling success. They are so starved for attention that they tend to be "proud" when they *do* get it.

Action Step: Write down one thing you are going to do, beginning today, to develop a better perspective in your relationship to God and others.

FAMILY OR PERSONAL PROJECT

This week, plan your family or personal devotional time around the subject of praise and thanksgiving. Read Psalm 150. Then make a list of things you have not thanked God for recently. Then spend time thanking Him for His blessings.

MOSES'
lesson in management

Have you ever been so overwhelmed with problems and responsibilities that you couldn't see your way out of them? Moses faced this dilemma in the wilderness. But God used someone, a very unexpected source, to give him a solution.

Once across the Red Sea, Moses led the children of Israel southward into the wilderness not by choice, but by God's direction. The northern route would have been a more logical choice, especially in view of two million people who would soon need food and water not only for themselves, but also for their herds and flocks. But the "cloud" moved southward (Exod. 13:17-22), and Moses, after his great declaration in his song of victory, was not about to take matters into his own hands. He had learned too much about God's presence, power, and leadership in his life.

But Moses' "wilderness school" experience was just beginning and little did he realize how much more he was going to learn about being an effective leader. True, he *had* come a long way. Psychologically, God had led him step by step in rebuilding his self-image.

And spiritually, Moses had learned to trust God and to act on that faith. In fact, it was the well-learned lessons in faith that enabled Moses to lead two million people directly into the wilderness, a maneuver that by human standards would be classified as irrational and irresponsible.

Ahead of Moses lay an awesome task. Imagine leading a mass of people two and one-half times the population of Dallas, Texas (or half the population of Chicago) into a wild and desolate desert, a wilderness where the natural resources for providing food and water were almost nonexistent.

And to make matters worse, the children of Israel were not noted for their spiritual maturity, which was all too obvious only three days later when they began murmuring and complaining because their water supply had run out (15:22-24). And in several weeks, in spite of God's marvelous provisions along the way, they were actually wishing that they "had died by the Lord's hand in the land of Egypt" rather than to be free from their bondage.

But one of Moses' greatest lessons in working with people came sometime later—after he had returned with the children of Israel to the very place God had first spoken to him from a burning bush. The place was Mount Horeb, designated as the "mountain of God" (3:1; 18:5). Here Israel was camped when Moses' father-in-law, Jethro, came to see Moses, bringing with him Moses' wife and two sons.

MOSES' FATHER-IN-LAW—GOD'S INSTRUMENT

Jethro, Moses' father-in-law and also the priest of Midian, had heard about Israel's miraculous deliverance from Egypt. And when Israel came in the direction of his own country, Jethro, in an act of love, took Moses' wife and children and went out to meet Moses (Exod. 18:1-7).

Jethro's Conversion

Though Jethro had heard generally about God's miraculous intervention for Israel, Moses soon filled him in on the particulars (18:8). Jethro's response to Moses' report must have been as rewarding to Moses as some of the great miracles he had observed on the way from Egypt to Mount Horeb.

And the miracle that Moses observed in his father-in-law's life was what the other miracles were all about: to demonstrate to those who do not know God that He *is* God. In short, it appears that Jethro was converted. He, like Abraham of old, put faith in God as the one true God and the only Saviour of mankind. And it was by faith in God that Jethro, too, was justified and made righteous in God's sight.

The Scriptures record that when Jethro heard about "all that the Lord had done to Pharaoh and to the Egyptians for Israel's sake" (18:8), he "rejoiced" (18:9). He blessed the Lord and testified: "Now I know that the Lord is greater than all the gods" (18:11). And the final step in his conversion experience, actually the confirmation, was an act of worship. He offered a burnt offering and sacrifice to the one true God (18:12).

Jethro's Observation

The day following his reunion with Moses and his conversion to God, Jethro had occasion to observe Moses' activity as leader of Israel. What he observed concerned him greatly. All day long Moses dealt with problems that existed among the people of Israel. One after another they came to Moses to get advice and counsel on how to solve their personal, family and social problems (Exod. 18:13-16). By the end of the day Moses was exhausted, and many of the Israelites were still frustrated because they had been standing in line all day long without an opportunity to communicate with Moses.

"The thing that you are doing is not good," observed Moses' father-in-law. "You will surely wear out, both yourself and these people who are with you, for the task is too heavy for you; you cannot do it alone" (18:17,18).

What a significant contrast! Some years before, in this very area, God patiently but persistently communicated with Moses from a burning bush, attempting to convince him that He wanted Moses—and him alone—to lead Israel out of Egypt. And when Moses refused to respond to God's call, the Lord reluctantly provided him with Aaron to be his spokesman and assistant. And as we've seen, God later helped Moses to rebuild his self-image and to become the sole leader of Israel, the one who took full responsibility for their leadership out of Egypt.

Moses learned that lesson well. But now, several years later, Moses was still trying to do the job of leading Israel all by himself. But he had another significant lesson to learn. His experience in Egypt had

84

been a much different situation, calling for a different style of leadership. Multiple leadership was not God's plan for communicating with Pharaoh. Furthermore, God's further plan was to exalt Moses, to build his image in the sight of both the Egyptians and Israel, to prepare him for the great task of leading Israel out of Egypt into the Promised Land.

But now, leading two million people through an uncharted wilderness called for a new style of leadership. Holding his hand in the air and waving his staff over the people of Israel was not God's plan for solving their social and interpersonal problems. It has never been God's plan to work this way with people. Moses had to learn how to handle this new kind of situation, and his newly converted father-in-law was God's instrument for communicating that new lesson.

Jethro's Suggestion

Jethro's suggestion to Moses was brilliant—so brilliant that certain aspects of this suggestion have even been used as a management model by management specialists in today's business world.

Jethro's proposal had three facets. *First, he suggested that Moses serve as a mediator between the people and God.* This was to be his primary responsibility, his priority. He was to spend time seeking God's will for the people (Exod. 18:19).

Second, once he determined God's will, he was to communicate God's will to the people. "Then," said Jethro, "teach them the statutes and the laws, and make known to them the way in which they are to walk, and the work they are to do" (18:20).

Third, he was to delegate responsibility to qualified men who could help him solve the day-by-day problems which the people faced in forming their new society and culture. Listen to Jethro's suggestion: "Furthermore, you shall select out of all the people able men who fear God, men of truth, those who hate dishonest gain; and you shall place these over them, as leaders of thousands, of hundreds, of fifties, and of tens" (18:21).

These newly appointed leaders were to handle the regular problems, the minor matters, and only the major problems were to be brought to Moses for his wisdom and counsel (18:22,23). "This plan," implied Jethro, "will enable you to survive the pressures of your leadership task, and will also make it possible to meet the needs of the children of Israel."

MOSES' FOLLOW-THROUGH

Moses did as his father-in-law suggested (Exod. 18:24-27). And the plan worked. In fact, the organizational structure that emerged to solve their social problems also became a very workable plan for thwarting military attacks from their enemies.

Moses had learned another significant lesson in his growth towards maturity, a lesson in management. Though God desired to use him, and him alone, in Egypt and in leading the people across the sea, his plan from that point onward was a *shared* responsibility. Moses learned that social problems are usually not resolved miraculously. Rather, they are solved through careful and painstaking communication and counseling. And Moses also learned that it is impossible for one man alone to do that kind of job.

MANAGEMENT LESSONS
FOR THE TWENTIETH-CENTURY CHRISTIAN

There are many lessons that all Christians can learn from this unusual experience in Moses' life. Let's look at just four.

We Must All Establish Priorities

There are too many demands upon every Christian to be able to do everything, and do them well. This was Moses' problem. It was utterly impossible for him to do everything by himself. He had to establish priorities.

For the Christian, there are significant priorities that we must establish to be in the will of God:

First, we must not neglect our relationship with God. And God's plan for that relationship to grow and mature is to have three vital experiences—learning the Word of God, having vital relational experiences with God and with other believers and having vital experiences sharing Christ with those who do not know Him (Acts 2:42-47). It is only as we engage in these New Testament experiences that we will become mature in Christ, both as individuals and as a body.

Second, we must not neglect our families. Our relationship with God, other believers and non-Christians should *never* replace or become a substitute for leading our families into the same kind of experiences. The Word of God is clear regarding our responsibility to our families (1 Tim. 5:8).

Third, we must not neglect our business responsibilities. There is no place in the Christian life for neglecting to be a good steward of our time when working for others. Again, listen to Paul: "Whatever you do, do your work heartily, as for the Lord rather than for men; knowing that from the Lord you will receive the reward of the inheritance. It is the Lord Christ whom you serve" (Col. 3:23,24).

Management Ability Is a Mark of Spiritual Maturity

In 1 Timothy 3 and Titus 1, Paul lists the marks of a mature man of God. And one of those marks is management ability. Note! A man who is seeking leadership in the church "must be one who manages his own household well, keeping his children under control with all dignity (but if a man does not know how to manage his own household, how will he take care of the church of God?)" (1 Tim. 3:4,5).

Delegation of Responsibility Must Be to Qualified Individuals

This is a truth we see all the way through the Scriptures wherever we see the appointment of leaders. Imagine what would have happened if Moses had selected immature men to help him, men who were not trustworthy. They would have multiplied his problems a thousandfold. This is why Paul puts such a strong emphasis on appointing men to church leadership who measure up to certain standards of maturity.

Understand, of course, that no one is perfect. No Christian has "arrived" in his Christian life. But there *is* a recognizable level of maturity. Otherwise Paul would not have set forth those qualities in 1 Timothy 3 and Titus 1 as a criteria for measuring maturity.

No Matter What Our Spiritual Maturity, We Must Always Be Open to Advice and Counsel

At this point in his life, Moses had become a very mature man of God, both psychologically and spiritually. But there was yet more to learn. And it took "a Jethro," a new believer, to help him learn a very significant lesson in how to be a *better* leader.

No Christian must ever get to the place where he is unteachable. If he does, he has ceased to be mature. There is always more to learn about God's plan for his life. Lessons often come from very unexpected sources.

And let's conclude with another significant reflection of maturity in Moses' life. Moses' receptivity to his father-in-law's suggestion was that reflection. As we've all experienced, the most difficult people to receive advice from are often those closest to us, those within our own family structure. Moses demonstrated true humility when he listened objectively to his father-in-law and followed what proved to be expert advice.

LIFE RESPONSE

Select the area in your life that you feel you need to give the most attention to in becoming a more mature Christian, and then write out the first step you are going to take to begin to achieve this goal.

☐ Establishing priorities;

☐ Developing my management abilities in my home, in the church and in the business world;

☐ Learning to delegate responsibility to qualified people;

☐ Being open to advice and counsel from *any* source God wants to use.

Now write out the first step you are going to take in achieving this goal.

FAMILY OR PERSONAL PROJECT

Read together Acts 6:1-7. Compared with Moses' experience in Exodus 18, what are the similarities of the apostles' experience in Jerusalem?

MOSES'
greatest test

Have you ever faced a test so great you felt you couldn't bear it another minute? This was already the theme of Moses' life, but his greatest test came at Sinai.

The next great experience for Israel, and Moses, was at Mount Sinai. And what an experience! It was Israel's first *direct* encounter with God. Heretofore, the Lord had revealed His words through Moses. At Sinai, the children of Israel heard God's voice directly. And it was at Sinai that Moses experienced his greatest test as a leader, a test that, ironically, related to Israel's greatest rebellion.

Before we look at that rebellion and test, let's review. It is important to remember that before Israel was delivered from Egyptian bondage, the world was almost totally given over to idolatry and immorality. Generally speaking, mankind had forsaken God. The cyclic process of spiritual degeneration and deterioration—which is so graphically described by the

91

apostle Paul in his letter to the Romans, and which once resulted in the flood—had once again taken place.

Men, who at one time "knew God ... did not honor Him as God" and "they became futile in their speculations, and their foolish heart was darkened." Eventually, they "exchanged the glory of the incorruptible God for an image in the form of corruptible man and of birds and four-footed animals and crawling creatures." And correlated with this deterioration came another predictable phenomenon, flagrant immorality. Thus Paul wrote that "God gave them over in the lusts of their hearts to impurity, that their bodies might be dishonored among them" (Rom. 1:21-24).

GOD'S GRACE TOWARDS ISRAEL

But though all men had turned against Him, God in love began the process of redemption by choosing one man, Abraham, out of the pagan masses. He made Abraham a promise: that He would give him and his descendants a land, that He would make him a great nation, and that through him all the families of the earth would be blessed (Gen. 12:1-3).

There is one thing about God—He cannot lie—no matter how fickle, dishonest and immoral man becomes. And in leading Israel out of Egypt, God was in the process of keeping His promise.

He had already welded Israel together through a tie of common parentage, common occupation and a common trial. And in *His* time, He had called Moses to be the great deliverer. Through the plagues, the Red Sea experience and the wilderness miracles, God was demonstrating to Israel, and to the world, that He was the one true God! God was reaching out to all mankind, inviting them to worship Him.

And then Israel came to Sinai, the place where God took His most loving and gracious step thus far. He actually revealed Himself to Israel directly—first, through lightning, thunder, smoke, fire and the sound of the trumpet. In fact, the "whole mountain quaked violently" (Exod. 19:16-19). And in the midst of this awe-inspiring phenomenon, God's voice could be heard by all Israel.

First, He told them that it was *He* who had brought them out of the land of Egypt! And then He spoke forth ten clear-cut and unmistakable commandments. And it was no accident that the first commandment condemned idolatry. "You shall have no other gods before Me," said Jehovah. "You shall not make for yourself an idol, or any likeness of what is in heaven above or on the earth beneath or in the water under the earth. You shall not worship them or serve them" (20:3-5).

During Israel's stay at Mount Sinai, Moses ascended the mountain numerous times and entered the very presence of God to receive additional instructions regarding the way God wanted Israel to worship Him and the way He wanted the children of Israel to treat each other (Exod. 20—24). On one occasion, Moses stayed 40 days and nights to receive God's instructions for erecting the Tabernacle (Exod. 25—31). And it was during this time that Israel—in the full light of God's love and grace which He had extended to them—reverted to almost incredible behavior.

ISRAEL'S INGRATITUDE TOWARDS GOD

It is difficult to understand Israel's actions at this moment in their history, unless we recognize from our own experience that man is inherently selfish and capable of the worst kind of ungrateful behavior. Still, if there is an extreme example of ungrateful behavior, certainly Israel is that example.

Note once again what God had done for Israel! They had witnessed the signs God had given to Moses when He first called him in the wilderness and sent him back to Egypt. They had experienced the ten plagues in Egypt and God's protective hand on them in the midst of these violent demonstrations of God's wrath and power. They had walked across the Red Sea on dry ground and then looked on with amazement as God destroyed the Egyptians in the midst of the sea.

During the wilderness journey they had heard Moses cry to the Lord on their behalf at Marah and then drank of the water that was turned sweet because of the tree Moses threw into the bitter pool. They had been eating the quail that God sent every evening, and were continually, even while at Sinai, feeding on the sweet manna that God sent every morning.

And later at Rephidim, they saw the unmistakable miracle when Moses struck a rock with his rod and it brought forth water. In this very place, they also experienced a supernatural victory over Amalek and his people because Moses held his hands towards heaven (here God is refreshing their memories as to how He had used Moses' *rod* and *hands* on previous occasions to deliver them from Egypt).

94

And now, at Sinai, they had seen the mountain quake, accompanied by lightning, thunder, fire, smoke and the sound of the trumpet. They had literally heard the voice of God warning them against worshiping false gods. And, on several occasions, they had witnessed Moses ascend and descend the mountain, entering the cloud to receive instructions from God. In fact, just before Moses had entered the cloud to stay for 40 days and nights, 70 elders of Israel, with Aaron and his sons, went up the mountain *with* Moses and saw a literal manifestation of God Himself (Exod. 24:9-11).

Yes, it is inconceivable that Israel at this moment would turn their backs on God. But they did! It is especially difficult to understand in view of God's efforts to reach out to Israel. Yet they spurned God's grace and engaged in incredible idolatry and immorality.

Israel's Rebellious Idolatry

Moses entered the presence of God and withdrew from Israel's vision for only six weeks. And sometime during this period the people grew restless. They began to doubt God's presence and power.

How they could do this is, from a twentieth-century perspective, beyond logical explanation. The fiery cloud was still there. They were eating the miraculous manna every morning. Just several weeks before they had heard God speak.

Nevertheless, they fashioned the image of a "god" made with human hand from their own material possessions, one they could see and worship. And what is more difficult to understand, Aaron, the brother of Moses, the one who participated in performing the miracles in Egypt, succumbed to Israel's demands to make this "graven image." (See Exod. 32:1-6.)

It is important to note that Israel was not denying God's existence. Rather, they wanted some "representative" of this God of Abraham, Isaac and Jacob that they could see and touch. Moses had temporarily disappeared. And with his absence came a restless desire to create this representative, to make an animal idol in which God would dwell. This, of course, was a reversion to the pagan practices they had learned in Egypt, and an abomination to Jehovah. But here also is an ancient illustration of how easy and "natural" it is for people raised in a pagan environment to mix pagan religious practices with true religious practices.

It was very illogical and demeaning, of course, to believe that God would cooperate with such a plan—especially in view of His repeated warnings regarding the danger of *even approaching* the holy mountain because of His great holiness and majesty (Exod. 19:21-24). But make the calf they did! They offered sacrifices to this graven image, ate and drank as a part of their religious ritual, and engaged in open and degrading immorality. With this behavior they were participating in the very practices of heathen religions where immoral behavior was a vital part of their religious worship.

God's Righteous Indignation

The Lord's reaction to Israel's abominable actions is explicitly recorded in the Scriptures (Exod. 32:7,

96

8). "I have seen this people and behold, they are an obstinate people," said the Lord. "Now then let Me alone, that My anger may burn against them, and that I may destroy them" (32:9,10).

There is no question that God was ready to destroy all of the children of Israel from off the face of the earth. His patience had run out. In view of all that He had done to reach out to Israel, to reveal His power, to teach His laws and to make known His love and care, He was now very angry with their flagrant rejection.

This was also a great test for Moses. One of the most significant lessons he learned emerges from this passage. God made it very difficult for His servant: "I will make of you [Moses] a great nation" (32:10). In other words, God told Moses He was ready to start over, to wipe out the people He had brought out of Egypt and to fulfill His promise to Abraham through Moses' immediate family.

What a great temptation this would provide for any ordinary person! Here once again was Moses' opportunity to become the center of human history. And here was Moses' greatest test!

Moses' Relentless Intercession

But Moses passed the test! In fact, his maturity was overwhelming, especially in the light of his previous spiritual and psychological problems. Moses immediately became a true and loyal mediator between the people and God. He wasted no time in interceding for the children of Israel (Exod. 32:11). He pleaded with the Lord on their behalf and reminded Him of His original purpose in bringing Israel out from bondage

97

—to demonstrate His great power before the Egyptians (32:12). He also reminded the Lord of His promise to Abraham, Isaac and Jacob (32:13).

This event, more than any other to this time in Moses' life, demonstrated that his growth and development since that day God spoke to him from the burning bush was remarkable. His maturity was reflected this time through his love for Israel. A couple of years before, he was not even willing to leave the wilderness to help deliver Israel from bondage. Now we see him pleading to God to save Israel, and, as we'll see, even offered his own life along with Israel if God would not restrain His wrath.

Through this direct and open communication with God, Moses succeeded in changing God's mind (something we can't really understand). We're told that "the Lord changed His mind about the harm which He said He would do to His people" (32:14). But evidently God did not reveal this to Moses immediately. He allowed Moses to go down to the people and to confront them with their sin, to destroy the molten calf and to confront Aaron with his irresponsibility. (See 32:15-21.)

Aaron's reaction to Moses' confrontation was almost humorous—a lesson to us all! His rationalization was a classic example of man's tendency towards self-deception and dishonesty. Note what must have been a very emotional dialogue between Moses and his brother: "Then Moses said to Aaron, 'What did this people do to you, that you have brought such great sin upon them?' And Aaron said, 'Do not let the anger of my lord burn; you know the people yourself, that they are prone to evil. For they said to me,

"Make a god for us who will go before us; for this Moses, the man who brought us up from the land of Egypt, we do not know what has become of him." And I said to them, "Whoever has any gold, let them tear it off." So they gave it to me, and I threw it into the fire, and out came this calf.' " (32:21-24).

"Out came this calf!" What an indication of a man with his back against the wall while being confronted with his irresponsible actions. The earlier record is clear that Aaron deliberately took the golden ornaments the people gave him and "fashioned it with a graving tool, and made it into a molten calf" (32:4). He had deliberately cooperated with their request to construct this idol and consequently was just as guilty as anyone in Israel of flagrant idolatry.

Note: Some believe that Aaron was trying to thwart Israel's attempts to construct an idol when he first requested them to give up their jewelry. The speculation is that he believed they were too selfish to take this step. But if this was his strategy, he completely miscalculated their response. The lesson, of course, is clear! Honest straightforward communication is always the best policy when dealing with sin.

Moses set out immediately to restore order among the children of Israel. Evidently, debauchery and sordid behavior existed everywhere throughout the camp. Again Aaron is blamed for this social and spiritual disorder (32:25).

Once order was restored (32:26-29), Moses again ascended the holy mountain to plead Israel's case, to try to change God's mind and to see if he could make atonement for their sins (32:30,31). As noted earlier, God had not yet revealed to Moses His willingness to withdraw immediate judgment upon Israel.

Moses' approach to God on Israel's behalf is an overwhelming lesson in pastoral love and concern. His actions defy all human explanation, for he made it clear to the Lord that he wanted to die with his people if they were not spared. "But now," pleaded Moses, "if Thou wilt forgive their sin—and if not, please blot me out from Thy book which Thou hast written!" (32:32).

CONSISTENCY, FICKLENESS AND THE TWENTIETH-CENTURY CHRISTIANS

Moses' example at Sinai is, of course, a beautiful picture of what Jesus Christ has done for us. Because of God's holiness and our sin, God cannot look upon us or allow us to come into His presence. We are all under the curse of death because of Adam's sin (Rom. 3:23; 6:23). But Jesus Christ, even when man rejected Him, went to the cross to die for all men's sins. In fact, He died for the sins of those who at that very moment were literally nailing Him to the cross.

Moses' Consistency

There is another great lesson in this passage from the life of Moses. In the events at Sinai, we see a demonstration of pastoral concern, "stick-to-itive-ness" and a commitment to people that was only superseded by that of Jesus Christ. How easy it would have been for Moses to turn against Israel at this point, to retaliate for their persistent criticisms and rejection of him during their wilderness journey. But he didn't. Even when the eternal God was ready to punish Israel, Moses remained true to Israel. He

100

pleaded their case, and even offered to die with them (Exod. 32:32-35).

There is no love greater than when a man is willing to die for his enemies. This Jesus Christ did, just as Moses was willing to do for Israel. But for Moses to have died would have been in vain, for only the perfect Son of God could be the one to make atonement for man's sin.

Have you accepted Jesus Christ's gift to you—the gift of eternal life? Have you put your faith in Christ's atoning work on your behalf at Calvary? If not, you are continuing to reject God's love and, as with Israel, eventually His patience and longsuffering will cease and He will have to judge all those who are still under the curse of sin.

How can you be saved? Paul gave the answer clearly and succinctly when the Philippian jailer asked the same question: "Believe in the Lord Jesus, and you shall be saved, you and your household" (Acts 16: 31).

Man's Fickleness

This Old Testament story also has another significant lesson, one that is particularly applicable to Christians. Generally, mankind has always been fickle. The history of the human race is one of taking God for granted and eventually turning away from Him. Even Israel, God's chosen people, has fallen into this trap again and again throughout their own history.

But Christians are guilty too! How easy it is to forget God's blessings! How short our memories are when it comes to remembering what God has done for us in the past! How quickly we complain when things don't go just the way we want them to! How easy it is to feel sorry for ourselves, even in the midst of material and spiritual blessings that surround us on every side. And how easy it is to rationalize our behavior, like Aaron, when we engage in irresponsible behavior and do not want to face our guilt!

LIFE RESPONSE

☐ Today I personally receive Jesus Christ as my Saviour. I am thankful He died for me on the cross, to take away my sin.

☐ Today I confess that I often take my spiritual and material blessings for granted. I confess that I far too often complain and murmur about things that I shouldn't. Lord, give me a positive attitude about life and help me to walk worthy of my high and noble calling in Christ. When I am discouraged, help me to count my blessings and to be thankful I am a Christian, living where I can worship and praise God in freedom and dignity.

FAMILY OR PERSONAL PROJECT

Conduct your own personal communion service with your family or friends, making it a time of thanking and praising God for His wonderful redemptive plan, as well as the spiritual and material blessings He provides you with every day.

MOSES
a friend of God

Those with great leadership responsibility often pay a great price! But there are also some great rewards, even on this earth. For Moses, it was his intimate relationship with God.

Israel had engaged in unbelievable idolatry—worshiping the golden calf—and God's anger had reached its zenith. The Lord was ready to wipe Israel off the face of the earth. But Moses, with a commitment to his people that was only superseded by that of Jesus Christ Himself, offered his own life along with theirs if God were to slay the children of Israel.

God's heart was touched by His servant's plea. And in an act of love that we can only accept and understand by faith, the sovereign Lord of the universe "changed His mind about the harm which He said He would do to His people" (Exod 32:14). "But," said the Lord, "I cannot let this sin go unpunished." Therefore, in the next two chapters of Exodus, we see God withdrawing His presence from

Israel, Moses' persistent prayer for Israel and God's renewed promise to Israel. All of this brings into sharp focus a picture of a man who is truly a friend of God.

GOD WITHDRAWS HIS PRESENCE FROM ISRAEL

Moses' previous prayer on behalf of Israel was that God might spare the children of Israel, forgive their sins and allow them to continue on into the Promised Land. God consented to save their lives, but He would not turn His back on their idolatry. The sin was too grievous. Therefore, God told Moses (Exod. 33: 1,2) to leave Sinai and go on up to the Promised Land—but, said the Lord, "I will not go up in your midst ... lest I destroy you on the way" (33:3). In other words, God would no longer manifest Himself to Israel as He had done from Egypt to this point in their journey, working miracles and personally dwelling among them.

Don't misunderstand! God is omnipresent and always has been. He is everywhere at all times. But He has chosen at certain times in history to make Himself known in unusual ways, to localize His presence through unusual manifestations. This He had done especially at Sinai.

When Moses reported God's decision to Israel, they were chagrined. Both inwardly and outwardly, they "went into mourning" (33:4). They removed their ornaments as God commanded; no doubt a symbolic act of repentance for using these items to fashion a false god (33:5,6).

But God, in His love, was still available to Israel,

to those who wanted to worship Him. Before the Tabernacle was ever constructed, Moses put up a tent outside the camp of Israel. There Moses would go to talk with God "face to face, just as a man speaks to his friend" (33:11). And the opportunity of going out to the tent was also open to anyone at all who honestly "sought the Lord" (33:7).

Thus we see God's grace once again. Though He had rejected Israel as a nation, He was still available to those individuals who sincerely wanted to do the will of God. And thus it has always been with God, for even today, in spite of the sins of all mankind, "whoever will call upon the name of the Lord will be saved" (Rom. 10:13). God is still reaching out to individuals, no matter how much mankind has rejected Him.

Moses, of course, had a particular place in God's heart. He had been called to be a mediator between Israel and God, and he faithfully discharged this responsibility, as we shall see in the verses to follow.

MOSES' PERSISTENT PRAYER FOR ISRAEL

Moses' relationship and friendship with God was obvious not only from his continued personal communion with the Lord, but also from his honesty and openness with Him. This of course was, and always has been, a mark of true friendship. Though Moses approached God with the greatest sense of awe and reverence, he also opened his heart and shared his deepest feelings of frustration and anguish. Thus the conversation between Moses and the Lord in verses 12-16 of Exodus 33, is a classic illustration of a human being communicating with the eternal and sovereign God in openness and candor—truly as friend with friend—and resulting in the influencing of God's actions.

God had told Moses that He would be *with him*—not *with Israel*—and he led the children of Israel to the Promised Land (33:14). And this frustrated Moses! Thus he said to the Lord: "If Thy presence does not go *with us*, do not lead us up from here" (33:15). In other words, Moses told the Lord he did not even want to go any further if God would not manifest Himself to Israel as well.

At this point, Moses' thinking is understandable. If Israel had rejected *God's presence and voice* at Sinai, what guarantee did Moses have that they would follow *him*, even though he was in direct touch with God? All previous evidence, of course, pointed to the fact that Israel's future apostasy was very predictable.

And then, too, hadn't God Himself given up on Israel? Thus Moses, in an honest but respectful way, reminded the Lord that He was asking him to do the seemingly impossible. "If they wouldn't respect *You* and respond to *You*, the all-powerful and miracle-working God of the universe," Moses implies, "then how will they respond to *me*, a mere man, whom they have rejected all along when things got a little tough."

And again we see the power in Moses' prayerful intercession for Israel. God's response was one of sympathy and understanding, for, said the Lord to Moses, "I will also do this thing of which you have spoken; for you have found favor in My sight, and I have known you by name" (33:17).

But Moses, with that reassurance from the Lord, took yet another daring step. "I pray Thee," he said, "show me Thy glory!" (33:18). With this request, Moses was asking God to reveal Himself more than ever before, to actually allow Moses to look upon His face. Though Moses had been communicating with God as a friend talks with a friend face to face, he had not yet ever caught a glimpse of God's face. And this he could never do, for to look at God in this way, to see the very essence of His glory and personality was impossible, for God's glory and holiness would be so overwhelming that no man could look and live.

But God had an alternate plan, another evidence of His love for Moses. "And He said, 'I Myself will make all My goodness pass before you, and will proclaim the name of the Lord before you; and I will be gracious to whom I will be gracious, and will show compassion on whom I will show compassion.' But He said, 'You cannot see My face, for no man can see Me and live!' Then the Lord said, 'Behold, there is a place by Me, and you shall stand there on the rock; and it will come about, while My glory is passing by, that I will put you in the cleft of the rock and cover you with My hand until I have passed by. Then I will take My hand away and you shall see My back, but My face shall not be seen' " (33:19-23).

And this God did! He invited Moses once again to come to the top of Mount Sinai. There He revealed Himself to Moses as He said He would (34:1-8). And in the midst of this glorious manifestation and Moses' holy communion, as he fell on his face and worshiped, he again voiced his prayer for Israel: "If now I have found favor in Thy sight, O Lord, I pray, let the Lord go along in our midst, even though the people are so obstinate; and do Thou pardon our

iniquity and our sin, and take us as Thine own possession" (34:9).

GOD'S RENEWED PROMISE TO ISRAEL

God, in His incomprehensible love for Moses and
the children of Israel, answered Moses' prayer and
renewed His covenant, but with a clear-cut stipula-
tion. He promised to be with Israel, to perform miracles in their midst which had never "been produced
in all the earth" (Exod. 34:10,11). But, said the Lord,
"Watch yourself that you make no covenant with the
inhabitants of the land into which you are going, lest
it become a snare in your midst" (34:12). God
warned Israel that they must destroy the false gods
of Canaan; that they must "tear down their altars and
smash their sacred pillars!" (34:13).

God made it very clear to Israel that He would
never again tolerate idolatry (34:14-17). Their idolatry would bring judgment on them and their children,
judgment that then was beyond their comprehension
(see Deut. 4:23-28). Unfortunately, Israel *did not*
remain true to Jehovah in spite of His grace and love
towards them.

Eventually, God's judgment fell and, down
through history to this very day, Israel has been rejected and hated by many people all over the world.
The hatred towards Israel by many Arab nations and
the twentieth-century Middle East crisis speak
dramatically of Israel's failure to follow God. Though
hatred and evil treatment towards the Jews is never
justified in God's sight, yet it is all a part of His
prophetic plan for Israel. Again we cannot understand this divine paradox, but then who has ever been

able to fully comprehend the infinite eternal God?

TWENTIETH-CENTURY PRAYER PRIVILEGES
The story of Moses communicating with God is the story of a man who had an unusual relationship with God. He feared God, but was unafraid; he was reverent, but honest; and he was respectful, but persistent.

In the Old Testament only a few men, like Moses, could ever enter God's holy presence. Today, few Christians fully realize how accessible God is to all those who know Jesus Christ. Listen to the writer of Hebrews: "Since then we have a great high priest who has passed through the heavens, Jesus the Son of God, let us hold fast our confession. For we do not have a high priest who cannot sympathize with our weaknesses, but one who has been tempted in all things as we are, yet without sin. Let us therefore draw near with confidence to the throne of grace, that we may receive mercy and may find grace to help in time of need" (Heb. 4:14-16).

Because of Christ's death and resurrection, because of His perfect sacrifice for our sins, we can come into God's presence any time and openly and honestly pour out our concerns and problems. Paul says: "Be anxious for nothing, but in everything by prayer and supplication with thanksgiving let your requests be made known to God" (Phil. 4:6).

It is wonderful that Christians need not go to a special place on a special day to worship God—although we are certainly commanded to regularly associate with other Christians (see Heb. 10:24,25). We need not even wear special clothes. We need not use certain words. We need not crawl on our hands and knees. We need not purify ourselves with certain rituals. We need not do any of these.

Rather, we can worship God anywhere—at home, at school or at work, while walking down the street, driving the car or quarterbacking a football game. We can call out to Him at any time and under any circumstance, whether working in a bank wearing a white shirt or digging a ditch wearing overalls.

And our words are not important either, for God understands simple sentences, complex sentences, big words, little words. In fact, He understands even when we don't use words at all. Paul says: "And in the same way the Spirit also helps our weakness; for we do not know how to pray as we should, but the Spirit Himself intercedes for us with groanings too deep for words; and He who searches the hearts knows what the mind of the Spirit is, because He intercedes for the saints according to the will of God" (Rom. 8:26,27).

And our posture and practice is not important either. We can talk with God on our knees, with hands folded and eyes closed. Or we can talk to God standing erect, looking towards heaven, with our hands held high and our eyes wide open. We need not engage in any ritual to get God's attention.

Jesus Christ has done everything that is necessary to allow us to come into God's most holy presence. And furthermore, we need not enter God's presence through any human priest, such as a "Moses" or an "Aaron." Thus Paul says: "There is one God, and one mediator also between God and men, the man Christ Jesus" (1 Tim. 2:5).

And most wonderful of all, we need not turn our faces away from God. Rather we can enter His very presence unafraid. Again the writer of Hebrews says clearly: "Since therefore, brethren, we have confidence to enter the holy place by the blood of Jesus, by a new and living way which He inaugurated for us through the veil, that is, His flesh, and since we have a great priest over the house of God, let us draw near with a sincere heart in full assurance of faith, having our hearts sprinkled clean from an evil conscience and our body washed with pure water" (Heb. 10:19-22).

LIFE RESPONSE

Following are various attitudes and actions that characterize many Christians. With which one do you identify the most:

☐ A fear of God that keeps me from approaching Him as a friend; or, at the other extreme, a flippant attitude that takes God's wonderful grace for granted.

☐ A fear of praying out loud because I'm afraid I'll not be able to use eloquent words.

☐ An attitude that I can only pray at certain times and in certain places.

☐ An attitude that judges people by what they wear and what they do when they worship God. (Note: This can go two directions. People with suits and ties are just as acceptable to God as those who dress more casually.)

☐ Additional attitudes I have that may not be in harmony with God's Word: (identify them).

111

FAMILY OR PERSONAL PROJECT

Discuss this message and life response with your family or friends. Particularly, read over the twentieth-century application and pay special attention to Scripture references that apply. Spend time thanking God for Jesus Christ and the wonderful salvation He has provided for everyone who receives Him as their personal Saviour.

MOSES'
greatest spiritual experience

Did you know that sometimes a great test or trial sets the stage for a great spiritual experience? Moses discovered this on several occasions during his lifetime, but particularly at Mount Sinai.

Israel's idolatry, the worshiping of a golden calf, was one of Moses' greatest tests! But this supreme trial set the stage for one of Moses' greatest spiritual experiences!

This is an important Old Testament lesson for all New Testament Christians to learn. For it is often the most difficult experiences that become the most significant opportunities for spiritual growth. Thus James wrote: "Consider it all joy, my brethren, when you encounter various trials; knowing that the testing of your faith produces endurance. And let endurance have its perfect result, that you may be perfect and complete, lacking in nothing" (Jas. 1:2-4).

113

In Moses' life, Israel's idolatry and hardness of heart towards God was the trial that opened up communication lines between Moses and God as never before. And these lines of communication reflected a very important flow pattern: from *Moses to God*, from *God to Moses* and from *Moses to the people*.

MOSES' COMMUNICATION WITH GOD

Prior to this time, God had, of course, been speaking to Moses and Moses with Him. But this trial—Israel's idolatry—stepped up the intensity of Moses' communication with God. On three successive occasions, Moses prayed earnestly for Israel as he had never prayed before, pleading with the Lord that He would cease being angry with them and withdraw His judgment.

Moses' First Request

While on the mountain with God, receiving the instructions for building the Tabernacle, Moses had "intreated the Lord" not to destroy Israel—while they were down below and, at that very moment, actually engaged in flagrant idolatry and immorality. (See Exod. 32:9-13.) And God, because He loved Moses, listened to Moses' prayer—even though His anger still burned against Israel—and "changed His mind about the harm which He said He would do to His people" (32:14). But, said the Lord, "I will not go up in your midst" (33:3).

In other words, the Lord would not destroy them, but He was going to withdraw His presence from them. This, of course, precipitated Moses' second urgent request for Israel.

114

Moses' Second Request

Once God promised that He would not destroy Israel, Moses then pleaded with the Lord to go with them—*not to withdraw His presence.* In fact, Moses argued with the Lord as he had in his first prayer. At first he said: "If Thou wilt forgive their sin—and if not, please blot me out from Thy book which Thou hast written!" (Exod. 32:32). And now, in his second prayer, Moses pleaded: "If Thy presence does not go with us, do not lead us up from here" (33:15). In other words, Moses was saying, "We might as well die right here—for if You don't go with us, Lord, we'll never make it anyway."

And once again, because the Lord loved Moses, He answered his prayer. "You have found favor in My sight," said the Lord to Moses, "and I have known you by name" (33:17).

Moses' Third Request

Moses' third request for Israel took place once again on top of Mount Sinai. Moses had asked to see the Lord's glory. And in the midst of a glorious manifestation of the Lord's presence, Moses took another bold step on behalf of Israel. Falling on his face before the Lord, he prayed: "Take us as Thine own possession" (Exod. 34:9). In other words, Moses was asking God to renew His covenant with them, to take them back once again as His special people, not only to be with them, but to manifest Himself to the world through them and to bring them into the land as He had promised Abraham He would.

Again God responded to Moses' prayer and said, "Behold, I am going to make a covenant. Before all

115

your people I will perform miracles which have not been produced in all the earth, nor among any of the nations" (34:10). "But," said the Lord, "you must never again become idolators—or you've had it!" (paraphrase of 34:11-16).

And with this final step of forgiveness, Israel, as a nation, was once again back in fellowship with the God they had openly rejected. Though they and several generations would still suffer the consequences of their sins, God renewed His covenant with Israel as a nation (34:6,7,10).

The impact of Israel's rebellion on Moses' prayer life is obvious! Like all of us, his communication with God was intensified in the midst of this difficult experience. It is a very normal process.

At this point, most of us can identify with Moses. As James said, in the context of instructing Christians regarding what their attitude towards trials should be: "But if any of you lacks wisdom, let him ask of God, who gives to all men generously and without reproach, and it will be given to him" (Jas. 1:5).

Unfortunately, some Christians never really pray until they're in trouble. This is natural. But for a person to become more intense in prayer during trials *is* very natural and part of the blessing that comes from experiencing difficult situations.

GOD'S COMMUNICATION WITH MOSES

Moses' intense communication with the Lord set the stage for the Lord to engage in more intense and significant communication with Moses. Once again, Moses stayed on top of Mount Sinai for 40 days and

116

40 nights (Exod. 34:27,28). During this period of time, God once again wrote the Ten Commandments on tablets of stone to replace the former tablets Moses had shattered when he had come down from the mountain, only to find the children of Israel worshiping an idol (34:1).

But this encounter with God was different, in that Moses observed more directly God's power and glory. When he came down from the mountain this second time, Moses' face literally reflected the glory of God (34:29). To date, this was Moses' greatest spiritual experience. God, in answer to Moses' prayer, had revealed to Moses as much of His glory as was possible without overcoming and literally destroying His servant.

MOSES' COMMUNICATION WITH THE CHILDREN OF ISRAEL

When the children of Israel saw Moses coming down from the mountain, they were immediately aware of God's presence in him. Thus we read that "when Aaron and all the sons of Israel saw Moses, behold, the skin of his face shone, and they were afraid to come near him" (Exod. 34:30). But once they understood what had happened, they gathered around Moses and listened intently as he transmitted to them the message he had received from God on Mount Sinai (34:31,32). And they willingly received the message, knowing that God was speaking through His servant Moses.

Interestingly, because of Israel's tendency to forget God—as they had done previously even in the midst of His glorious manifestations, Moses would put a

117

veil over his face when he was through speaking, so that the children of Israel would not see the glory of God fade away. And then, when he would go into God's presence, he would remove the veil and once again God's glory would be reflected in Moses' face. Then he would go out to speak to the people, once again reflecting God's presence to the people (34:33, 35).

A NEW TESTAMENT PARALLEL

The apostle Paul, in his second letter to the Corinthians, mentioned the experience Moses had on Mount Sinai during the second 40 days and 40 nights (see 2 Cor. 3:1-18). Though Paul was teaching several profound truths in this New Testament passage, there is one that is especially related to the fact that Moses, because of his relationship with God, reflected God's glory.

Contextually, Paul was defending his apostleship. And in doing so, he stated that the greatest proof of his divine appointment and ministry was the Corinthians themselves. Other teachers were carrying around letters of commendation and recommendation, but, said Paul, "you [Corinthians] are our letter, written in our hearts, known and read by all men; being manifested that you are a letter of Christ, cared for by us, written not with ink, but with the Spirit of the living God, not on tablets of stone, but on tablets of human hearts" (2 Cor. 3:2,3).

In other words, Paul was teaching that a New Testament body of Christians should reflect God's glory, just as Moses reflected God's glory when he received the Ten Commandments—and even more so! Paul

118

demonstrated this truth with a series of contrasts between the Old and the New Covenants (2 Cor. 3:7-9,11, italics added):

OLD COVENANT	NEW COVENANT
"But if the *ministry of death,* in letters engraved on stones, came with glory, so that the sons of Israel could not look intently at the face of Moses because of the glory of his face, fading as it was,	how shall the *ministry of the Spirit* fail to be even more with glory?" (3:7,8)
"For if the *ministry of condemnation* has glory,	much more does the *ministry* of righteousness abound in glory" (3:9).
"For if *that which fades away* was with glory,	much more *that which remains* is in glory" (3:11).

Paul culminated this Corinthian passage with a straightforward challenge to all Christians: "But we all," he wrote, "with unveiled face [like Moses in the presence of God] beholding as in a mirror the glory of the Lord, are being transformed into the same image from glory to glory, just as from the Lord, the Spirit" (3:18).

Just what does Paul mean? Though some aspects of this verse are difficult to understand, one thing is very clear; Christians are to continually become more and more like Jesus Christ, reflecting His glory. As we behold Him, as we look upon His face, as we see His image reflected in the Word of God, we are to be transformed into His very image. "Now we see in a mirror dimly," wrote Paul in his first Corinthian letter, "but then face to face" (1 Cor. 13:12). In other words, now we can only see a reflection of the Lord, but someday we'll see Him face to face and we shall be like Him. But in the meantime, the message is clear. We should be continually reflecting His glory, and more and more!

TWENTIETH-CENTURY LESSONS

There are several significant lessons for all Christians that grow out of Moses' greatest spiritual experience.

First, though it may be difficult at times, we must attempt to see the blessings inherent in various problems we face in life.

As we've already noted, James reminded us that we are to have a positive attitude towards trials because they test our faith and produce endurance, and endurance produces maturity (Jas. 1:2-4). Furthermore, if it were not for the problems and difficulties in our lives, we would tend to rely upon our own efforts and abilities. Trials and tests can draw us closer to God. Great tests can produce great spiritual experiences, experiences we may never have had if it were not for the difficulties of life. Thus Paul, too, writes that we should "exult in our tribulations; knowing that tribulation brings about perseverance; and perseverance, proven character; and proven character, hope; and hope does not disappoint" (Rom. 5:3-5).

Second, before we can communicate effectively with others, we must develop our own personal communication with God.

This was Moses' secret! After experiencing the glory and power of God in his own life, he was able to communicate that glory and power to Israel.

How well do you know God? And how well are you communicating your relationship with God to others? There is only one way to get to know God intimately, and that is through Bible study and prayer. Through the Word of God we discover God's thoughts, His character and His will for our lives. And through prayer we communicate with Him, getting to know Him by coming right into His very presence through the Lord Jesus Christ, our great high priest and mediator.

Third, Christians as a body are to reflect the glory of God. Interestingly, it was *individuals* like Moses in the Old Testament who reflected the glory of God. But in the New Testament, God's basic plan is that His *Body*, the Church, reflect His glory.

In fact, it is only the Body of Christ that can reflect certain aspects of Christ's life, such as the unity He had with the Father. Only the Body of Christ can reflect this particular aspect of Christ's life. No individual Christian can do it by himself.

Another example of an aspect that can only be reflected corporately is the fruit of the Spirit listed in Galatians 5:22,23. Frequently, we individualize this fruit, that is, attribute it to some individual Christian experience. But a careful study of the context of these verses will reveal that Paul is talking about fruit that is *relational* in nature. It cannot be reflected in isolation.

Thus we see that a local body of Christians that is growing and maturing in Jesus Christ will more and more reflect the image of Jesus Christ, becoming more and more like Him.

LIFE RESPONSE

Consider the following Scriptures. Select the one that you feel you are having the most difficulty applying to your life as a member of the Body of Christ. Spend a moment in prayer asking God to help you begin today to apply these Scriptures to your life.

☐ James 1:2-4: "Consider it all joy, my brethren, when you encounter various trials; knowing that the testing of your faith produces endurance. And let endurance have its perfect result, that you may be perfect and complete, lacking in nothing."

☐ 2 Timothy 2:15: "Be diligent to present yourself approved to God as a workman who does not need to be ashamed, handling accurately the word of truth."

☐ 1 Thessalonians 5:16-18: "Rejoice always; pray without ceasing; in everything give thanks; for this is God's will for you in Christ Jesus."

☐ John 13:34,35: "A new commandment I give to

you, that you love one another, even as I have loved you, that you also love one another. By this all men will know that you are My disciples, if you have love for one another."

FAMILY OR PERSONAL PROJECT
Share your life response with your friends or other members of your family. Share particularly how you plan to apply these Scriptures to your life in a specific way. Then spend time praying for one another, asking God to help you carry through.

MOSES'
depression

Can a Christian ever become depressed, so depressed he wants to die? Moses did! And there was a reason—in fact, several! And the most exciting dimension to this story is God's solution.

Israel camped at Sinai for one year. And a lot happened, both to Israel and to their leader, Moses. Here the children of Israel committed their greatest sin, worshiping the golden calf. And here Moses passed his greatest test, his relentless intercession for Israel's forgiveness.

At Sinai, Israel received God's law—not only the moral law as embodied in the Ten Commandments, but also the laws of God which were to govern their civil and religious life as well. And here Moses engaged in communication with God such as no man had ever before experienced. He talked with God face to face, as friend with friend. In fact, all 27

124

chapters of Leviticus and the first nine chapters of Numbers record God's words to Israel through Moses while the people were encamped at Sinai. The statement, "Then the Lord spoke to Moses, saying . . . " (or a similar one) appears nearly 60 times in these chapters.

But the day finally came for Israel to move on, to leave Sinai and travel on towards the Promised Land (Num. 10:11-13). The cloud that hovered over the Tabernacle suddenly began to move, and Moses and all Israel knew it was time to break camp and follow the Lord (see also Exod. 40:34-38). And so they did! But Moses, in spite of his optimistic attitude at this time, was still not ready to cope with what transpired just three days after they left Sinai. I'm not sure any man would be! Most important, however, God understood Moses' problem.

ISRAEL'S CONTENTION

Moses was optimistic when they broke camp. He seemed to be highly motivated, no doubt because of his personal communion with the Lord over the past 12 months and Israel's positive response to the Word of God. This optimism is seen in his prayer to the Lord when they left Sinai: "Rise up, O Lord!" shouted Moses. "And let Thine enemies be scattered, and let those who hate Thee flee before Thee" (Num. 10:35).

Then it happened! It was like tearing open an old wound, one that had been healed over. In fact, the timing was uncanny and ironic. Just three days after leaving Sinai (Num. 10:33), Israel began to complain (Num. 11:1), just as they had done three days after

125

they had sung Moses' song of victory following their marvelous deliverance from the Egyptians when they crossed the Red Sea (see Exod. 15:22-24).

And to make matters worse, Israel had *less* to complain about than previously, and they had a far greater knowledge of God's Word and will for their lives. When they first complained at Marah, they had no water to drink, but this time there was no lack. At Marah, God had not spoken directly to Israel, but this time they complained in the full light of God's revelation which had come thundering from Sinai.

And the Lord wasted no time showing His displeasure towards Israel, "His anger was kindled, and the fire of the Lord burned among them and consumed some of the outskirts of the camp" (Num. 11:1). And with this act of grace, God was keeping His promise to Moses not to destroy suddenly all Israel from off the face of the earth. Rather, the Lord sent out a warning to those who were complaining.

Moses responded to this situation well. He once again interceded for Israel and God harkened to his voice. "The fire died out" (11:2).

But Moses was not emotionally prepared for the next event. Many of the sons of Israel ignored God's gracious warning and began to complain *again* about their plight. "Who will give us meat to eat?" they whined. "We remember the fish which we used to eat free in Egypt, the cucumbers and the melons and the leeks and the onions and the garlic .... There is nothing at all to look at except this manna" (11:4-6).

It was not a matter of having *no* food! Rather, they wanted *better* food! They were not satisfied with God's generous provision of manna, His glorious presence in the Tabernacle and His gracious promise that He would eventually bring them to the land of Canaan, to a land of plenty that would make Egypt's vegetables and fruit seem as nothing. No, the children of Israel had already forgotten God and what He had done for them—just three days after a tremendous year at Sinai. Think of it! Just three days! How self-centered and forgetful man can be!

MOSES' DEPRESSION

The renewed complaining of the people threw Moses into a state of extreme frustration. He felt the weight of the whole problem resting squarely on his own shoulders.

To say the least, "Moses was displeased" with the total situation (Num. 11:10). In fact, his conversation with the Lord makes it quite clear that he was ready to give up, to quit. And several things Moses said reflect the symptoms of a person who is terribly distressed and anxious about his ability to cope with the demands that he thinks God is about to put on him.

Moses Lost Sight of God's Promises

He thought God had forsaken him, and he took God's judgment of Israel very personally. Listen to his prayer: "Why hast Thou been so hard on Thy servant? And why have I not found favor in Thy sight, that Thou hast laid the burden of all this people on me? Was it I who conceived all this people?" (Num. 11:11,12).

Then Moses said something to the Lord that gives us a significant clue as to what he must have thought God was going to do when He turned a deaf ear towards Israel. "Was it I," asked Moses, "who brought them forth, that Thou shouldest say to me, 'Carry them in your bosom as a nurse carries a nursing infant, to the land which Thou didst swear to their fathers'?" (11:12).

Moses thought God was going to leave him with the total responsibility of leading Israel into the land. He knew how frustrated and angry God was with Israel for their past and present sins. So it was only natural for him to assume that God was forsaking them, that he alone would have to bear the burden.

Moses, like most of us in a crisis situation, forgot God's promises both to himself and to Israel. "My presence shall go with you," God had said to Moses (Exod. 33:14). And to Israel He had said, "I am going to drive out the Amorite before you, and the Canaanite, the Hittite, the Perizzite, the Hivite and the Jebusite" (Exod. 34:11). There were no "ands," no "ifs" and no "buts" about their initial possession of the land. God was going to do it. He had definitely renewed His covenant with Israel. But even though God had made a promise, somehow in the midst of a dark moment, Moses forgot it.

Moses Lost Sight of God's Power

"Where am I to get meat to give to all this people?" Moses asked the Lord (Num. 11:13). And later, even after God had told Moses He would give them meat —so much they'd be sick of it, he still had difficulty believing God was able to do it. Thus Moses said to the Lord, "The people, among whom I am, are 600,-000 on foot; ... Should flocks and herds be slaughtered for them, to be sufficient for them? Or should all the fish of the sea be gathered together for them, to be sufficient for them?" (11:21,22).

Then God had to remind Moses, even Moses, of His strong and mighty arm. "Is the Lord's power limited? Now you shall see whether My word will come true for you or not" (11:23).

Interestingly, Moses may not have been doubting God's power to supply the food. Rather, perhaps he was voicing his opinion that even if God supplied all the fish in the sea, it would not be enough to satisfy Israel. In other words, nothing could satisfy this group of people, no matter how much was given them. They simply would not be satisfied.

But whatever Moses meant, in his state of weariness and depression he lost sight of what God had done for Israel on many previous occasions. This is not unusual, for most of us experience similar emotions when we are tired, distraught and facing many pressures of life.

Moses Lost Perspective of God's Overall Plan

"I alone," said Moses, "am not able to carry all this people, because it is too burdensome for me" (11:14).

God, of course, had never told Moses he would have to do it all by himself. Rather, He had promised Moses, ever since the burning bush, that He would be with him and help him.

But in this moment of distress and despair, Moses' memory faded. What he *knew* suddenly seemed to be lost in a mass of emotions and feelings so overwhelming that he wanted God to take his life. If God were going to forsake him, Moses wanted to end it all—

right then and there! "Please kill me at once!" he cried out to God (11:15).

This, of course, was not God's plan. And the most encouraging aspect of this story is that God understood His servant's feelings of resentment and despair. After all, God Himself was so distraught over Israel that He felt like destroying them. So why shouldn't God understand Moses, a mere human being, who was experiencing at least some of the same feelings that God Himself was feeling.

Loss of perspective in a time of great stress, even by some of God's choicest servants, is not a new phenomenon. Elijah once experienced these same emotions. After God, by working great miracles, had granted him great victories over God's enemies, Elijah fled into the wilderness, sat down under a tree and asked God to take his life.

God's response to Elijah's need at that moment is another great lesson. He put Elijah to sleep, then awakened him and fed him. He then put Elijah to sleep again, and once again God awakened him and fed him. Elijah then traveled on, refreshed and strengthened. In fact, the Bible says he "went in the strength of that food forty days and forty nights" (1 Kings 19:8).

God's response to Elijah was just what he needed. He knew His servant was totally exhausted, emotionally, physically and spiritually, especially after his great confrontation with the 450 prophets of Baal. So God met his need accordingly—in this case with food and rest. Well, God understood Moses just as He understood Elijah. And, as He had on many previous occasions, God provided the solution for Moses.

GOD'S SOLUTION

God's solution to the problem Moses faced was twofold (Num. 11:16-33):

First, He met Moses' need. God instructed him to select 70 men from the elders of Israel whom he knew personally, men who were already doing a good job. Moses was to bring them to the Tabernacle. "Then," said the Lord, "I will come down and speak with you there, and I will take of the Spirit who is upon you, and will put Him upon them; and they shall bear the burden of the people with you, so that you shall not bear it alone" (Num. 11:17).

This God did (11:25). He knew Moses needed encouragement and help. He knew that what Moses had to do was humanly impossible to do alone. And so He anointed 70 other men who could help Moses bear the burden of his leadership position.

The second aspect of God's solution was that He brought judgment upon Israel. The people asked for meat, and God gave it to them. In fact, He gave them so much they got sick. They were greedy, and God brought judgment upon them for their greed and ungrateful attitude.

"While the meat was still between their teeth, before it was chewed, the anger of the Lord was kindled against the people, and the Lord struck the people with a very severe plague" (11:33).

Interestingly, God recognized that Moses had legitimate reasons for his distress, unhappiness and complaints. But He also knew that Israel's attitudes were totally unjustified. Consequently, God had compassion on Moses, but He judged Israel.

DEPRESSION AND
THE TWENTIETH-CENTURY CHRISTIAN

There are several significant lessons that emerge from this Old Testament event. But let's zero in on just one—Moses' depression. There are at least three things we can learn from Moses' experience.

First, it is important to know what happens to Christians when we get depressed. Like Moses, we tend to forget God's *promises* and His *power*, and we lose *perspective* of His *plan* for our lives. No matter how close we have been to God in the past, no matter how many times He has answered our prayers, no matter how clear our perspective and how exciting our lives, we can hit a low point that literally "wipes us out." In fact, during times of unusual stress it is not uncommon to think the thoughts Moses and Elijah thought, that is, "I'd rather be dead."

These factors are the *results* of depression, not the *cause.* Christians frequently confuse the two. In both Moses' and Elijah's life, the cause that led to depression was *stress.* The result was inability to think, feel and act properly.

Second, it is important to realize that God understands our depression. He knows our plight, our predicament, our feelings of totally being "out of it." He understood Moses, He understood Elijah, and He understands us. He knows we are but human beings. He knows our weaknesses. He knows that we sometimes get tired and frustrated, and sometimes fearful, sometimes angry.

And like Moses and Elijah, we can lay our hearts bare before Him. If we feel like dying, we can tell Him so! And He understands!

132

Third, we must seek God's solution to the problem of depression. If we get depressed because of sin in our lives, we need to deal with that sin. There is no other solution. We need to confess it to God, ask forgiveness from others if we have wronged them and then with God's help, continue to do the will of God.

However, not all depression is caused by specific sin in our lives. The problem Moses faced which led to depression was one that even God had difficulty tolerating. And Elijah—well, he exerted so much energy and experienced so much stress doing God's work that he was on the verge of a nervous breakdown. In each case, God's solution was different, but effective.

Why, if not from specific sins against God, do Christians get depressed?

Some Christians get depressed as a result of feeling guilty about things for which they should not feel guilty. That is, they have not sinned against God's Word but against false, man-made standards. But whether it is true guilt or false guilt, it will still cause depression. Christians need to tune their consciences to the Word of God, not to false standards.

Some Christians get depressed as a result of physical problems; for example, glandular imbalance. If a Christian cannot isolate a particular cause for depression he should get a physical examination from a competent medical doctor. In recent years there have been unbelievable break-throughs in treating depression that has physical, rather than mental or spiritual, causes.

Some Christians get depressed as a result of their environment. For example, some women are cooped

133

up all day at home with their children. If this goes on day after day without a break, depression is inevitable. The only way to overcome this problem is to get away, to change their environment, to take a break from the demanding routines of life.

Christian men often get depressed as a result of the demands of their work: fighting the problems in a rat-race society, counseling with people about their problems, hassling with other human relations problems. Again, every Christian needs periodic breaks from these pressures.

Some Christians get depressed because they don't use common sense. They overwork, they plan poorly, overextend themselves and set goals that are too high. What must a Christian do about these problems? Though God understands our dilemmas in life, for the most part we must take action to help ourselves overcome these problems.

And remember! Depression with its accompanying guilt, is made worse through self-condemnation. If depression is caused by sin, settle it with God—today! His solution is the shed blood of Jesus Christ that cleanses us from all unrighteousness.

If depression is brought on by other causes, realize that God understands. Don't condemn yourself! But remember that you and I are responsible, with God's help, to find the solution to our problems and to act on that solution.

LIFE RESPONSE

If you identify with this chapter, particularly Moses' depression, ask God to help you isolate the basic cause of your problems. Use the above points as a checklist. Then with a friend—your husband, your wife, your pastor—work out a solution.

FAMILY OR PERSONAL PROJECT

Read the book, *Guilt and Freedom*, by Bruce Narramore and Bill Counts (Vision House). This is an excellent book that will further help you to isolate the true causes of guilt and depression in the Christian life.

MOSES
faces unjust criticism

Personal criticism that is justified is one thing! To be sure, it is always hard to take. But criticism that is unjust is doubly difficult to handle—especially if it comes from those who should have the most understanding. This was Moses' dilemma.

Moses had already fought a lot of personal battles with Israel—their complaining, their idolatry, their immorality! But no one yet had attacked him personally, questioning his motives and accusing him of thinking that he was something special, accusing him of pride and self-exaltation, blaming him for the judgment that God brought on Israel.

But it happened. This was one of the next major tests and trials that Moses faced. And as you read and study his life, you really wonder how much stress and turmoil one man can take. Moses—or any man—would have given up long ago if he had faced these struggles all alone.

But God had promised Moses He would never leave him—and He never did. In fact, the moment the Lord heard these unjust criticisms, He moved into action and did something about it. And for the most part, He did so before Moses ever responded in self-defense.

As you read through the biblical account, you will notice an interesting sequence: *First, Moses was hit from within his own immediate family,* by his own brother and sister. *Second, he was undercut by his own leaders,* men he had chosen and had confidence in. *And third, he was falsely accused by the whole congregation,* by all the sons of Israel who were sold a bill of goods by self-seeking men.

UNJUST CRITICISM FROM HIS FAMILY

Criticism that hurts the most is criticism that comes from those closest to you, especially if it's unfair and unjust criticism. And when Miriam and Aaron, Moses' own sister and brother, accused him of pride, thinking he had a more important leadership position than they, it must have crushed him.

The picture, of course, is clear. Miriam and Aaron were jealous. Jealousy is a motive that often causes people to strike out at others unjustly. And for obvious reasons, the real motive for their criticism was camouflaged, at least at first.

Aaron and Miriam followed a very interesting strategy. They at first "spoke against Moses because of the Cushite woman whom he had married" (Num. 12:1). No doubt Zipporah, Moses' first wife, had died, and he had remarried. And this was not wrong, for the woman, though not an Israelite, was surely a believer. If she had not been, God Himself would have judged Moses. True, God had warned against marrying pagans, but He was not opposed to mar-

137

riage between men and women who were true believers no matter what their background.

But Miriam and Aaron took it upon themselves to chide Moses, to judge him for his action, no doubt to try to demonstrate to Moses—but primarily to others —that they too, like Moses, were capable of telling others what was right and wrong. Thus, they followed their initial speech with the real reason they were condemning Moses: "Has the Lord indeed spoken only through Moses? Has He not spoken through us as well?" (12:2).

If Miriam and Aaron had approached their brother privately, it would have been easier for Moses to bear the criticism. But this approach, of course, would not have achieved their purpose. Aaron and Miriam were really not concerned about Moses; they were concerned about themselves. They wanted others to know that they too were capable of leading Israel. They wanted more of the spotlight. So they made their accusations public, using Moses' marriage to a Cushite as a basis for demonstrating their wisdom before others, thus trying to prove that they, too, had special favor with God.

Moses' response to this false criticism immediately revealed who was right and who was wrong. Self-defense is not necessarily wrong, but there are times when it's better to let the truth win out in other ways. In this case, Moses did not defend himself. Because of his humility and his meekness, he did not try to justify himself or to put his brother and sister down (12:3). He knew he was being falsely criticized, and that the truth would become evident. And of course it did!

God stepped into the scene immediately, no doubt before Moses even cried out for help. He honored Moses' response, his humility, his meekness, his willingness to bear this false accusation without a counterattack. God dealt with Aaron and Miriam, first by making it very clear to them that they were not on the same level as Moses. True, Miriam was a prophetess and Aaron was a high priest, but God only spoke to them through visions and dreams. But with Moses, God said, "With him I speak mouth to mouth, even openly, and not in dark sayings, and he beholds the form of the Lord" (12:8).

God became angry with Aaron and Miriam for their selfishness and self-centered behavior. "Why then were you not afraid to speak against My servant, against Moses?" He asked (12:8). And because Miriam had instigated this plot against Moses, the Lord struck her with leprosy (12:9,10).

Interestingly, Aaron had once again demonstrated a very serious weakness in his personality. He was more of a follower than a leader. At Sinai, he had succumbed to Israel's pleas to build a golden calf, and then rationalized his behavior when he was confronted with his sin (Exod. 32:24). Now he had followed Miriam's suggestion to criticize Moses. No doubt he was not only a weak leader, but he lacked discernment as well. This, of course, makes his attack on Moses' leadership ability even more ridiculous and foolish.

But Aaron's reaction to God's judgment on his sister also revealed a tender heart—a quality of spirit. Combined with his weakness was a strength. He confessed his sin (Num. 12:11) and demonstrated immediate concern for his sister (12:12). No doubt, he was also motivated by guilt and fear—a fear that he too might be struck with the same affliction. But there is also an element of true repentance in his behavior. And God honored that element, slight as it may have been.

Moses' reaction, however, is even more significant. He held no grudges! Furthermore, he did not take the opportunity to demonstrate to Israel the "wrong-ness" of their behavior and the "rightness" of his. If he had been an opportunist, looking for a chance to build himself up, to defend himself, here it was. Miriam was leprous "white as snow" (12:10), and Aaron was trembling on his knees, begging for mercy. What a timely occasion for self-defense, and in front of all Israel.

But Moses, man of God that he was, "cried out to the Lord, saying, 'Oh God, heal her, I pray' " (12:13). And God responded to Moses' prayer—after allowing Miriam to remain in her condition for seven days outside the camp. In other words, God made things right for Moses, while all Israel remained camped in that place until Miriam was healed. Israel looked on, I'm sure, with fear in their own hearts, and most significantly, they looked on with a new appreciation for Moses. God had truly defended His servant against false accusations.

UNJUST CRITICISM FROM HIS FELLOW-LEADERS

As usual, Israel's memory was very short. They seemed to forget lessons as fast as they learned them. In fact, after they had finally arrived in Kadesh and had sent spies into Canaan, they wanted to turn back to Egypt because of the spies' report (Num. 13:1—14:4). So they once again experienced God's judgment on them for their unbelief as they wandered in the wilderness (14:5-45).

Then, after all this, a certain group of leaders still had the gall to falsely accuse Moses. Obviously, they had also conveniently forgotten or ignored the episode when Miriam and Aaron were judged by God for jealous behavior and for false accusations against Moses. This time Korah, a descendent of Levi and one of Moses' trusted leaders, was the instigator. He influenced three other leaders—Dathan, Abiram and On—to rebel. They in turn influenced 250 other "men of renown," to join them in a conspiracy against Moses (Num. 16:1,2).

Once the rebels formulated their plan, "they assembled together against Moses and Aaron [this time Aaron was accused along with Moses—perhaps a dose of his own medicine], and said to them, 'You have gone far enough, for all the congregation are holy, every one of them, and the Lord is in their midst; so why do you exalt yourselves above the assembly of the Lord?' " (16:3). With this accusation, these men were making it quite clear to Moses and Aaron that everyone else in Israel was "just as holy" as they. Interestingly, they worded their criticism very carefully, involving the whole "congregation" in the accusation.

No doubt, these leaders had gone from tent to tent, building up the ego of all the people. Their story probably went something like this: "Moses and Aaron think they're something special. They think

that they're the only ones who can represent us before God in the Tabernacle. You and I are just as holy
as they are. See, I am your leader, too, and I am not
exalting myself above you. Now listen, we're going to
have a confrontation with Moses. And we're going to
tell it like it is. And we want your backing, because
you're just as important as anyone."

Little did the people realize what a serious error
they were making to join this conspiracy. Eventually,
some of them were going to suffer serious judgment
by the Lord.

But we're getting ahead of the story. When Moses
heard this accusation, he was dumbfounded—so
much so "he fell on his face" (16:4). How could it be?
He and Aaron were simply following the instructions
of the Lord, not their own desires.

In fact, if God had let Moses have his own way, he
would have given up his leadership role a long time
ago. Think of the many times Moses had pleaded for
the lives of the Israelites—even offering his own life
as a ransom for theirs. And think how traumatic it
must have been for Moses to see leaders he had chosen and trusted twist the truth because of jealousy.

But Moses, man of God that he was, was quick to
regain perspective. He turned the problem over to the
Lord immediately and sought God's will in the matter. And God showed Moses how to deal with the
problem at the core. Thus Moses went right to Korah,
the instigator (16:5-7). And his words to this man and
his fellow Levites are very revealing: "Then Moses
said to Korah, 'Hear now, you sons of Levi, is it not
enough for you that the God of Israel has separated
you from the rest of the congregation of Israel, to

bring you near to Himself, to do the service of the Tabernacle of the Lord, and to stand before the congregation to minister to them; and that He has brought you near, Korah, and all your brothers, sons of Levi, with you?' " (16:8-10).

Now the picture is very clear. As a Levite, Korah was jealous. He wasn't satisfied with his already select position in Israel—he wanted more. And he infected many others with his self-centered motives. To achieve his goal he needed support; so he went out to get it. And through subtle and ego-building words, he got it.

God's solution to this problem was the most dramatic of all. The Lord caused the earth to open up and to swallow "Korah and company" (16:11-34). Furthermore, the 250 men who conspired against Moses with Korah were also destroyed, but by fire that came forth from the Lord while they were trying to demonstrate to everyone that they were just as holy as Moses and Aaron (16:35).

Once again, God had defended His servant Moses. When his good was evil-spoken of, the Lord extended His grace, even in the midst of His anger. (Read Num. 16 carefully and you will see God's grace all the way through, giving opportunity for repentance.) Also, God's judgment finally fell on those who insisted on defending their false motives and continuing in their sinful behavior.

UNJUST CRITICISM
FROM ALL THE SONS OF ISRAEL

The homework that Korah and his fellow rebels had done with the whole congregation of Israel paid off, but with a strange twist. The very next day, following God's judgment of the leaders of Israel, "all the congregation of the sons of Israel grumbled against Moses and Aaron, saying, 'You are the ones who have caused the death of the Lord's people'" (16:41).

God's anger was so stirred up against Israel, because they blamed Moses and Aaron for this judgment, that once again He was ready to destroy all Israel (16:42-45). But Moses, bless him, again began to intercede for the people—the very ones who falsely accused him. Even though judgment fell in the form of a severe plague on 14,700 of the people, a rather ironic thing happened! The majority were saved from this plague because Moses and Aaron made atonement for Israel's sin, burning incense before the Lord (16:46-50).

In other words, Moses and Aaron used the same rites that the 250 men tried to use before the Lord when the Lord destroyed them. But Moses and Aaron did the work God had told them to do, and they saved the majority of Israel from death. Furthermore, Moses' and Aaron's high calling as priests of Israel—which was under attack in the first place—was also defended by their obedience. When God defends a person against unjust criticism, He does it as no man can.

A NEW TESTAMENT CORRELATION
The writer of the book of Hebrews gives us an unusual insight into Moses' life, motives and place in history. We read: "By faith Moses, when he had grown up, refused to be called the son of Pharaoh's

daughter; choosing rather to endure ill-treatment with the people of God, than to enjoy the passing pleasures of sin; considering the *reproach of Christ* greater riches than the treasures of Egypt; for he was looking to the reward" (Heb. 11:24-26, italics added).

All the pain and suffering that Moses endured for the Lord during his lifetime can certainly be classified as identification with Christ's suffering, but the ill-treatment that we've observed in Numbers 12—16 is certainly unique and very closely correlated with Christ's experience on earth.

Let's back up a moment, however, to get a little larger picture of how Moses' life was symbolic of Christ's. Remember that Moses had all the privileges of royalty, being the adopted son of Pharaoh's daughter, and was actually heir to the throne of Egypt. But he gave it up to be identified with his own people, to become their deliverer and saviour. Jesus Christ, "who, although He existed in the form of God, did not regard equality with God a thing to be grasped, but emptied Himself, taking the form of a bond-servant, and being made in the likeness of men" (Phil. 2:6,7). Christ, too, was willing to give up His royal position to be identified with His people, yes, to be falsely accused and rejected by those closest to Him.

First, Jesus Christ, like Moses, was rejected by members of His own family. Even His brothers did not accept Him as the promised Messiah (John 7:5).

Joseph, too, is another beautiful illustration of one who was symbolic of Christ, for he was sold into Egypt by his 11 brothers. And their primary motivation was *jealousy.* They hated their brother Joseph because their father favored him. (See Gen. 37.)

How painful it must have been for Christ to be rejected by those closest to Him.

Second, Jesus Christ, like Moses, was rejected by the leadership of Israel.

The Pharisees and Sadducees and other religious leaders in Israel were His greatest enemies. They were threatened by His presence. And again, their primary motivation was *jealousy.* In fact, on one occasion after the Lord had raised Lazarus from the dead, they said: "If we let Him go on like this, all men will believe in Him, and the Romans will come and take away both our place and our nation." And, "so from that day on they planned together to kill Him" (John 11:48, 53).

How it must have hurt Jesus Christ to be rejected by the very ones who were to be the spiritual leaders of Israel.

Third, Jesus Christ, like Moses, was rejected by all Israel.

John writes, "He came to His own, and those who were His own did not receive Him" (John 1:11).

His own people, God's chosen people, the children of Israel as a nation, rejected Jesus Christ. But not only was He rejected by Israel, but also by us, for Pilate stands as our representative, washing his hands of the responsibility of allowing Jesus Christ to go to the cross. We must always remember that it was the sin of the *world* that nailed Jesus Christ to the cross.

But there is another significant correlation that we must never forget, a lesson that emerges from Moses' life. Again and again, when God's servant had been rejected and falsely accused by his people, he fell on his face and prayed that God would save their lives.

146

And how representative of Jesus Christ! When all had forsaken Him, He looked on them with compassion and said, even of His persecutors, "Father, forgive them; for they do not know what they are doing" (Luke 23:34).

UNJUST CRITICISM
AND THE TWENTIETH-CENTURY CHRISTIAN

Paul said, "Have this attitude in yourselves which was also in Christ Jesus" (Phil. 2:5). What is your response to unjust criticism? To rejection? To persecution? How easy to respond with resentment, self-defense and to return evil for evil. On another occasion, Paul told us to "Never pay back evil for evil to anyone" (Rom. 12:17). And again he said, "Never take your own revenge," but rather, "leave room for the wrath of God" (Rom. 12:19).

Does this mean a Christian should never defend himself? Not at all. Even Moses did (Num. 16:15). But he did it God's way, with God's direction and in God's will. Moses never paid back evil for evil, for he recognized, as we must, that only God can punish a man for his sin.

LIFE RESPONSE

Evaluate your attitudes lately. What is your response to unjust criticism? (Make sure it's *unjust*!) Sometimes we experience *just* criticism, because of our own mistakes. This we deserve!

Have you thought recently about the price that was paid for your redemption? Have you thought about the One who suffered unjust criticism and rejection to give you eternal life? Spend a moment in quiet

147

worship, thanking God for the Lord Jesus Christ.

And if you have never received Him personally as your Saviour, do so today. Invite Him to be your Deliverer from sin. Remember that Jesus Christ is the greatest gift that has ever been given to man. Have you received that gift, the gift of eternal life? Remember the words of the apostle John, who wrote, "But as many as received Him, to them He gave the right to become children of God, even to those who believe in His name" (John 1:12).

FAMILY OR PERSONAL PROJECT

Review this chapter together and then read Philippians 2:1-11. Then spend time thanking God for the marvelous gift of Jesus Christ, the Saviour of the world.

Numbers 20:1-13; 27:12-23; **13**
Deuteronomy 34:1-12

MOSES' final days

Does a person ever get too old and too wise to fail?
The answer is, of course, "No." And perhaps this is one
of the greatest lessons we can learn from Moses.

When Israel first came to Kadesh-barnea, God had
instructed Moses to send men to spy out the land of
Canaan—not to see if they could take the land, but
rather to develop a proper perspective on the situation (Num. 13:2). Out of the twelve who went into
the land, all agreed it was a great land—a land flowing
with milk and honey. But unfortunately, only two,
Joshua and Caleb, felt they could conquer the land.
The other ten were very fearful and reported of
large cities that were fortified and of the military
strength of the people who lived there. Their fear was
so great that it infected the whole nation. Very short-
ly, all Israel was in utter despair and refused to obey
the Lord. When Joshua and Caleb tried to convince

149

them that they should enter the land, the Israelites became so angry and frustrated they wanted to stone them, along with Moses and Aaron.

And then, suddenly, "the glory of the Lord appeared in the tent of meeting to all the sons of Israel" (Num. 14:10). And once again, God's judgment fell. And once again, Moses interceded for Israel. Rather than destroying them utterly, the Lord extended His grace and sentenced Israel to 40 years wandering in the wilderness, a year for every day the spies were in the land. They were to wander aimlessly until all those 20 years old and upward died, all those who had witnessed and rejected the Lord's gracious manifestations and miracles (Num. 32:11,12). There were to be only two exceptions—Joshua and Caleb, because they were obedient to the Lord (Num. 14:22-30).

And now 40 years are nearly past, rather uneventful years from the standpoint of the biblical record. This, too, seems significant, for not only was it a *wilderness* experience from an environmental point of view, but a barren and unfruitful existence for Israel personally and spiritually. It was basically characterized by "disobedience" and "dying" and by the growth and development of a new generation to replace the old that was under God's judgment because of their sin of unbelief.

But even during this time God did not forsake Israel, even though they forsook Him and continued to worship false gods (Amos 5:25,26; Acts 7:42,43). In spite of their idolatry, God met their physical needs. In retrospect Moses reminded them, "These forty years the Lord your God has been with you; you

150

have not lacked a thing. Your clothes have not worn out on you, and your sandal has not worn out on your foot" (Deut. 2:7;29:5).

What was going through Moses' mind during these years, we really don't know. We can only speculate. But whatever his thoughts, one thing is clear! He remained faithful to the Lord, and he did not forsake Israel. He accepted the judgment on Israel and lived and bore it with them, even though he was not party to their unbelief.

But perhaps he, too, began to experience the problem of forgetfulness during this barren experience. Perhaps the mighty power of God he had witnessed so frequently began to fade in his own memory. Perhaps he began to slip back into some of his old patterns of behavior. Moses was human, and 40 years wandering in the wilderness is a long time. And perhaps this will help us understand his actions towards the end of that 40 years when the new generation cried out for water in the wilderness of Zin.

MOSES' SIN

Israel was back in Kadesh. They had come full circle. It was the first month of the fortieth year. And they were without water (Num. 20:1,2). No doubt many of them were too young to remember what God had done at Rephidim when Moses struck the rock with his rod and water gushed forth (Exod. 17:1-6). And even if they had remembered, this new generation was following closely in the steps of their parents—murmuring, complaining and forgetting the blessings God was showering upon them daily (Num. 20:3-5).

151

Both Moses and Aaron, as they had done so many times before, went into the Tabernacle to pray for Israel (20:6). And God, as He had done so many times before, gave an answer to Israel's predicament. "The Lord spoke to Moses, saying, 'Take the rod; and you and your brother Aaron assemble the congregation and speak to the rock before their eyes, that it may yield its water' " (20:7,8).

For the most part, Moses and Aaron obeyed God explicitly. They took the rod, and assembled Israel before the rock (20:9). *But then* they departed from God's specific instruction. "Listen now, you rebels; shall we bring forth water for you out of this rock?" (20:10). And then Moses, rather than just speaking to the rock as God had said, struck the rock twice (20:11).

Several things happened at this moment in Moses' life that displeased the Lord. *First, he was obviously angry to the point where he lost control.* Interestingly, this is what he did when he first left Pharaoh's court to go out to deliver Israel from bondage. In a fit of anger, he struck down an Egyptian—an irresponsible act that plagued him for the next 40 years.

Second, Moses took matters into his own hands and deliberately disobeyed the Lord. Moses, who had been so cautious and particular about obeying God in every detail, in a moment of weakness failed to follow the Lord's instructions.

Third, Moses exalted himself and Aaron in front of Israel. "Shall *we* bring forth water?" he asked. Why Moses, the great and humble Moses, did this is difficult to discern. Perhaps he had begun to slip spiritually in his own relationship with God during the 40

152

years in the wilderness. Time has a way of dulling our sensitiveness to the Lord. Or perhaps he felt a need to demonstrate his position and power with God to this new generation. After all, most of these people would not have directly remembered the Red Sea, Marah and Sinai, and the many miracles God wrought through Moses.

But whatever the reason, Moses failed God at this moment. And the Lord could not overlook it. Not because He did not want to forgive His beloved servant, but because of the bad example Moses had set before all Israel. To allow Moses to get by with this sin without punishment would only encourage a weak and carnal Israel to disobey and doubt God even more than they already had. Therefore, God held Moses responsible and told him he would not be able to lead His people into the land (20:12; 27:12-14).

MOSES' MATURE RESPONSE

Moses' reaction to God's discipline was reflective of the man he *really* was! All men make mistakes, but only a man of God responds maturely when he's confronted with his mistakes. To be sure, Moses was disappointed. In his humanness, he pleaded with God to withdraw His judgment. "O Lord God," he prayed! "Thou hast begun to show Thy servant Thy greatness and Thy strong hand; for what god is there in heaven or on earth who can do such works and mighty acts as Thine? Let me, I pray, cross over and see the fair land that is beyond the Jordan" (Deut. 3:24,25).

But God would not assent to Moses' request. And

Moses immediately faced reality! He sensed God's determination. No doubt he remembered at this moment that many times he had, through prayer, been allowed to influence God's actions, to cause the Lord to withdraw His judgment on Israel. No doubt he was tempted to remind God that He had forgiven Israel for sins far greater than his own!

But not Moses! Rather, he turned his eyes away from himself and focused his attention once again on Israel. His primary concern was their welfare. What would they do without a leader? They would be like "sheep which have no shepherd" (Num. 27:17). "Appoint a man over the congregation," he prayed (27:16).

This prayer God answered! Joshua would be the man. And Moses must have been very pleased with God's choice for this young man—who was not so young now—had stood by him as no other, all the way from Egypt to the border of Canaan. There was no evidence of jealousy, no bitterness that often creeps in when younger men replace older men. Rather, Moses, the greatest of all Old Testament prophets, was willing to step aside and allow God to let Joshua lead Israel.

MOSES' DEPARTURE

Though Moses was not allowed to lead Israel into the land, God *did* partially answer his prayer—He allowed him to *see* the land (Deut. 34:1-4). In fact, God Himself conducted Moses on a guided tour to the top of Mount Pisgah, and there, from one of the highest peaks called Nebo, God showed Moses the land of Canaan (34:1-3). "This is the land which I

154

swore to Abraham, Isaac and Jacob saying, 'I will give it to your descendants'; I have let you see it with your eyes, but you shall not go over there" (34:4).

And then Moses died (34:5, 6). And though he "was one hundred and twenty years old when he died, his eye was not dim, nor his vigor abated" (34:7). Moses had begun his career in Israel as a strong and virile man; and even though he endured stress beyond what often seemed humanly possible, he ended his life on earth well preserved—a tribute to his trust and confidence in God.

Moses had no ordinary funeral. Most people are buried by other men. Moses was buried by the God of the universe. Some feel he was actually translated bodily to heaven like Elijah, who was taken to heaven in a whirlwind (2 Kings 2:ll).

But whatever the circumstances surrounding Moses' death and burial, it was glorious. And Moses went to spend eternity with his heavenly Father, where he would never make another mistake. There he would be eternally rewarded for his faithfulness as a leader of Israel. And there, too, he would never face another moment of anger, sorrow, unjust criticism or disappointment.

The sons of Israel mourned and wept over Moses' death for 30 days (Deut. 34:8). But the Lord's final tribute to Moses is astounding. In fact, Moses probably had one of the most significant epitaphs in history. And it is recorded not on a lonely tombstone in a secluded mountain cave but in the eternal Word of God: "Since then no prophet has risen in Israel like Moses, whom the Lord knew face to face, for all the signs and wonders which the Lord sent him to perform in the land of Egypt against Pharaoh, all his servants, and all his land, and for all the mighty power and for all the great terror which Moses performed in the sight of all Israel" (34:10-12).

Thus we discover that in spite of his human hang-ups and problems, Moses was—except for Jesus Christ—the greatest man of God who ever lived.

THE TWENTIETH-CENTURY CHRISTIAN— NEVER TOO OLD TO FAIL

Perhaps the greatest lesson we can learn from Moses' final days is that a person never gets too old to fail. No matter how close we have been to God, no matter how many answers we have had to prayer, no matter how much God has used us, we can still, in a moment of weakness, sin against God. Put another way, a faithful and successful life does not guarantee we will not blow it in the homestretch.

Therefore we must be on guard against Satan and his subtle attacks at all times. Interestingly, following a rather extensive account of Israel's many and successive failures, Paul exhorted the Corinthians: "Therefore let him who thinks he stands take heed lest he fall" (1 Cor. 10:12). But Paul also followed this exhortation with a glorious promise: "No temptation has overtaken you but such as is common to man; and God is faithful, who will not allow you to be tempted beyond what you are able; but with the temptation will provide the way of escape also, that you may be able to endure it" (1 Cor. 10:13).

Man need not fail. God has provided a way out. But we as Christians must walk through the door of escape. Avoiding sin is an act of the will. Thus Paul said to the Corinthian Christians, relative to their particular problem, "Therefore, my beloved, *flee* from idolatry" (1 Cor. 10:14, italics added).

LIFE RESPONSE

This "Life Response" is designed to be a brief review of Moses' life and an opportunity to reconfirm your desire to become a more mature Christian. Read over the statements and check those that indicate the lessons that have affected your life the most:

☐ Like Moses' parents, I want to be a wise and discerning father (or mother), one who has *faith* in God, *courage* to always do what is right, and a parent who has developed a careful *strategy* to rear my children in God's ways (Exod. 2:1-10).

☐ Like Moses, I want to make the right choices in life, choices to serve God and to put Jesus Christ at the center of my life, no matter what the cost (Heb. 11:24-26).

☐ I want to learn from Moses' mistakes; to be motivated more by reason than by emotion; to avoid trying to do God's work in my own strength; to avoid having to suffer rejection because of my own foolish mistakes (Exod. 2:11-15; Acts 7:23-29).

☐ I often identify with Moses' inferiority complex on the backside of the desert. But by God's grace, I want to respond to God, realizing that He can use me in spite of my human weaknesses (Exod. 2:23-25; 3:1-22; 4:1-20).

☐ As Moses allowed God to rebuild his self-confidence, I too want to allow God to rebuild mine, no matter how painful the process (Exod. 4:27—14:31).

☐ Like Moses, I always want to honor and glorify

God for all my successes in life (Exod. 15:1-18).

☐ I too, like Moses, want to learn to become a good manager of my own household as well as in any other area of responsibility (Exod. 18:1-27).

☐ When everyone around me is inconsistent and fickle, I want to be a faithful and consistent Christian, just like Moses was when all Israel turned to idolatry (Exod. 32:1-35).

☐ Like Moses, I want to develop my communication with God, realizing that He is my friend (Exod. 33:1-23).

☐ Like Moses, I want my life to reflect the glory of God because I spend time listening to His voice from the Scriptures and obeying what He says (Exod. 34:27-35).

☐ I want, like Moses, to handle depression and disappointment as a mature Christian, not being guilty for things I shouldn't be, but to quickly confess my sins when I *am* at fault, and then accept God's perfect forgiveness (Num. 11:1-25).

☐ As did Moses, I want to learn to handle criticism—particularly unjust criticism—with a mature attitude, leaving it to God to judge and punish those who are at fault (Num. 12:1-16; 16:1-35).

☐ I want to constantly be on guard against failure in my Christian life, realizing that no matter how long I've been a Christian, I can, like Moses, fail God (Num. 20:1-13; Deut. 34:1-12).

PERSONAL OR FAMILY PROJECT

Over the next several days review each family or personal project. How well are you following through in realizing your goals?